A Culture of Collusion: An inside Look at the Mexican Press

A Culture of Collusion:
An Inside Look at the Mexican Press

Edited by

William A. Orme, Jr.

North·South Center Press
UNIVERSITY OF MIAMI

The mission of the North-South Center is to promote better relations and serve as a catalyst for change among the United States, Canada, and the nations of Latin America and the Caribbean by advancing knowledge and understanding of the major political, social, economic, and cultural issues affecting the nations and peoples of the Western Hemisphere.

 © 1997 The Committee to Protect Journalists

North·South Center Press Published by the North-South Center Press, University of Miami, and UNIVERSITY OF MIAMI distributed by Lynne Rienner Publishers, Inc., 1800 30th Street, Suite 314, Boulder, CO 80301-1026. All rights reserved under International and Pan-American Conventions. No portion of the contents may be reproduced or transmitted in any form, or by any means, including photocopying, recording, or any information storage retrieval system, without prior permission in writing from the publisher. All copyright inquiries should be addressed to The Committee to Protect Journalists, 330 Seventh Avenue, 12th Floor, New York, NY 10001, USA.

To order or to return books, contact Lynne Rienner Publishers, Inc., 1800 30th Street, Suite 314, Boulder, CO 80301-1026, 303-444-6684, fax 303-444-0824.

Library of Congress Cataloging-in-Publication Data

A culture of collusion: An inside look at the Mexican press / edited by William A. Orme, Jr.
    p. cm.
    Includes bibliographical references and index.
    ISBN 1-57454-012-2 (alk. paper)
    1. Freedom of the press — Mexico. 2. Government and the press — Mexico.
    3. Journalists — Mexico — Crime against.   I. Orme. William A., Jr.
PN478.M4C85 1996   96-37650
323.44'5'0972 — dc21   CIP

Printed in the United States of America, EB/NC

01 00 99 98 97   6 5 4 3 2 1

Contents

Overview: From Collusion to Confrontation

The administration of President Ernesto Zedillo is facing increasingly critical scrutiny from Mexican news organizations that are declaring their political and financial independence from the government. The editor, a former correspondent in Mexico who now serves as the executive director of the Committee to Protect Journalists, located in New York, examines how the traditional interrelationship between the state and the media is beginning to change — and argues that the continuing serious press freedom problems in Mexico have a political importance that goes beyond Mexico's borders.

Section I: The Print Media

Chapter 1
A Culture of Collusion:
The Ties That Bind the Press and the PRI

Veteran editor and columnist Raymundo Riva Palacio provides a detailed look at the inner workings of the Mexican press and its relation to the government. Riva Palacio challenges many conventional notions about the problems facing press freedom in Mexico in one of the most thought-provoking essays on the subject ever published by a senior Mexican newspaperman.

Section II: Broadcast News

Section III: Attacking the Messenger

Do Mexican authorities deliberately cultivate an atmosphere of intimidation? What was the response of the Salinas government and its predecessor to the many reported threats and attacks against reporters and editors? Lucy Conger reviews their records and analyzes the chilling effect on the local and national media of fears of violent reprisal. She examines recent incidents of attacks on journalists and examines the two most significant media murders in recent years: the 1984 assassination of muckraking columnist Manuel Buendía in Mexico City and the 1988 shotgun murder of Tijuana journalist Hector "Félix the Cat" Miranda.

The NAFTA debate in Washington focused attention on Mexican environmental and labor practices but touched only cursorily on the more fundamental issue of democratization. Constraints on press freedoms — arguably, the least democratic aspect of the Mexican political system — were overlooked entirely. The State Department's annual reports on human rights violations have consistently included critical accounts of Mexican government press controls and physical attacks on Mexican journalists. These reports are intended as guidance for U.S. congressional evaluation of foreign aid allocations and other economic agreements. Mary Moynihan, an attorney, analyzes these reports and argues that they provide a precedent for taking press freedom problems into account in the negotiation of international trade pacts.

In the Western Hemisphere in the last decade, only drug-ridden Colombia has produced more reported incidents of assaulted and murdered journalists. Yet in Mexico it has always been exceedingly difficult to corroborate such reports. Press accounts typically are inconclusive and contradictory, while professional investigations and prosecutions are rare because of the endemic failures of the Mexican criminal justice system. Joel Solomon explains why CPJ investigations usually cannot establish a clear probable link between these homicides and the victims' professions.

Epilogue

Leading Mexican political commentator Jorge G. Castañeda looks back critically at the Salinas administration's press strategy and skeptically examines prospects for top-down mandates for media reform.

Acknowledgments

This book grew out of a research project on the news media in Mexico by the Committee to Protect Journalists (CPJ), a nonprofit, nonpartisan organization based in New York and devoted to the defense of press freedom in all countries of the world. The intent of the project was to put into context the many specific violations of press freedom and the professional rights of reporters and editors that CPJ has documented and denounced in Mexico over the past decade. The project was funded by a generous grant from the John D. and Catherine T. MacArthur Foundation.

I would especially like to thank Woody Wickham and Elspeth Revere of the MacArthur Foundation, for their encouragement and support; Barbara Belejack, for her invaluable editorial assistance; Mira Gajevic, Anya Schiffrin, and Kate Houghton, for their organizational and logistical help; Avner Gidron, for his astute guidance of CPJ's research staff over the past three years; and Kathy Hamman and Ambler Moss of the North-South Center. Most of all, I would like to thank the contributors to this volume, whose insights, dedication and professional generosity made this work possible. As editor, I take full responsibility for any shortcomings, oversights or inadvertent errors in the text; credit for the work belongs wholly to the contributors.

The opinions and analyses expressed in this book are the views of the writers and do not necessarily reflect the views of the Board of Directors of the Committee to Protect Journalists or those of the North-South Center.

William A. Orme, Jr.
Executive Director, The Committee to Protect Journalists
New York City
October 1996

i

Overview:
From Collusion to Confrontation

William A. Orme, Jr.

Two unrelated incidents in September 1996 perfectly illustrated the problems and pressures that hinder the development of a truly independent Mexican press.

In Mexico City, a heavily armed police unit stormed the headquarters of the capital's largest-circulation broadsheet, the once reliably pro-government *El Universal*, with orders to arrest the publisher on tax evasion charges. The publisher fled; he later turned himself in, angrily protesting his innocence. Journalism associations around the world protested what seemed, at minimum, an indefensibly excessive display of force. The executive editor, alluding to his recent hiring of prominent political columnists known for their acerbic critiques of the ruling party, denounced what he called "a decision by the government to suppress (our) critical and committed editorial policy."

A few days later, in the poor, heavily Indian state of Oaxaca, the editor of the muckraking local weekly *Contrapunto* was abducted by hooded men who blindfolded and held him overnight while interrogating him about the sources and exact locales of his stories on leftist guerrillas in the region. He says he revealed nothing of consequence, though he feared for his life. His kidnappers, though they never identified themselves, comported themselves as trained police investigators, the editor said after his release the following day. State and federal authorities denied knowledge of the abduction and

---

William A. Orme, Jr., is executive director of the Committee to Protect Journalists. A former correspondent for The Washington Post *and* The Economist *in Mexico City, he covered Latin American economic and political affairs for 15 years. Mr. Orme is the author of* Continental Shift: Free Trade & the New North America.

promised to investigate. Tellingly, no one in government challenged the journalist's assumption that his abductors were state security agents acting under orders.

The kidnapping and interrogation of the *Contrapunto* editor fit a classic pattern of harassment of local journalists in Mexico's outlying provinces. Journalism in small cities and towns far from Mexico City can be a dangerous business, and local reporters often feel that they have as much to fear from law-enforcement authorities as they do from criminal gangs and corrupt political bosses. Local and federal police have been implicated in the deaths of many of the 20 reporters and editors who have been investigated by the Committee to Protect Journalists (CPJ) in Mexico over the past decade. The ruling Institutional Revolutionary Party (Partido Revolucionario Institucional — PRI) does not have the bloody death-squad record of many regimes to its south, but it has nonetheless looked the other way as low-level officials committed such crimes with seeming impunity.

By contrast, the siege of *El Universal* was a highly unusual move for a political system that has historically refrained from overt intimidation of the press in Mexico City and has carefully cultivated close relationships with traditionally cautious mainstream papers like *El Universal.* Making this particular publisher the target was doubly surprising, as he had long been seen — like most Mexican newspaper owners — as a cooperative and well-rewarded member of the governing elite. The huge amount of his alleged tax bill — more than $5 million — only reinforced the impression that his purse had been fattened with official help.

Fairly or not, few local observers doubted that the government could make tax evasion charges stick. Virtually all leading Mexican businessmen are cynically assumed to have violated myriad provisions in the arcane and erratically enforced tax code, and news media owners are believed to have been treated with special leniency by state auditors over the years. *El Universal*, a paper that fattened its classified-ad revenues with paid government advertising and political tracts, but had only rarely engaged in probing reportage, had been seen by feistier rivals as a classic example of a paper that pulled punches in return for financial favors. Now that it was taking a more independent stance, the tax men had come calling, fronted by a phalanx of riot troops. It was hard to escape the conclusion that the government was quite deliberately demonstrating its continuing willingness to use its power to intimidate and control the daily press. Even if *El Universal's* publisher was being held out as a purported symbol of the corrupt cronyism of previous regimes, as some political observers suggested, the timing of this targeting still made the move seem like a direct reprisal against the paper's newly critical editorial voice.

There is good news as well as bad in these two incidents. The very fact that a staid daily like *El Universal* would begin turning on its former patrons was a testament to the increasing competitiveness and independence of the city's newspaper business. Editorially aggressive new rivals were threatening to overtake *El Universal* in the marketplace, and *El Universal* — a bastion of the old journalistic order — was belatedly asserting its own political independence in order to survive the challenge.

In Oaxaca, meanwhile, *Contrapunto* — barely a year old at the time — is emblematic of a new breed of crusading provincial newsweeklies that neither advertisers nor distributors would have touched a decade ago. And their crew of young reporters is typical of a new generation of Mexican journalists who acerbically question authority and refuse to act as the ruling party's paid scribes. That career path is not without risks, as the Oaxaca incident illustrated. But not long ago it would have been almost unthinkable in Mexico's poor rural states, where strong-arm governors, entrenched local bosses and sophisticated criminal gangs had been accustomed to considerable autonomy and almost complete freedom from journalistic scrutiny. The fact that ordinary Oaxacans can now read independent local reporting on armed insurgents in their own state is a potent symbol of how Mexican journalism is becoming a force for official accountability and social change.

Yet these remain exceptions to the still-prevailing rule of coercion and corruption by officials and the willing collaboration of many editors, publishers and broadcasters. The "Culture of Collusion" depicted in this book's lead essay is beginning to crack under the strains of Mexico's political and economic crises. An increasingly urban and angry electorate is demanding real reporting and spurning news services that peddle state propaganda. But the traditional press culture of Mexico and the government apparatus that sustains it are remarkably resilient and will not be reformed overnight.

It is the business of the Committee to Protect Journalists, where I work as executive director, to document and denounce specific abuses against press freedom: a journalist thrown in jail, a newspaper censored, a reporter attacked or murdered. Over the years we have reported scores of such incidents in Mexico. Yet we have always been acutely aware that press freedom violations can only be fully understood in the context of the political system and press culture in which they occur.

And the incidents alone only tell part of the story. The central question of the prospects for real press freedom can only be answered by stepping inside the country's newsrooms and examining the daily pressures and problems faced by working journalists and their news organizations. The essays in this volume were commissioned in an effort to illuminate those issues in detail and, more broadly, to shed light on a critical but little-understood aspect of Mexico's political system.

In the United States, the long debate over the North American Free Trade Agreement (NAFTA) focused overdue attention on Mexican political culture.

Concerns were raised about labor rights, environmental problems, electoral practices, the independence of the judiciary, the protection of civil liberties. But little attention was paid to the issue of press freedom, which is fundamental to the workings of any democratic society.

Understanding the Mexican press is a key to understanding Mexico. This book examines how newspapers routinely tailor their coverage in exchange for state subsidies, advertising revenues and payment for the front-page placement of specific news stories. We explain why television news has presented a monolithically pro-government view of events, with dissenting viewpoints only recently getting exposure under brokered election-reform agreements.

Most disturbingly, this book chronicles a pattern of violence against journalists that continues to this day. Since 1984, at least 10 journalists have been killed because of their reporting, and scores more have been attacked or harassed by national police and other security forces. Only a few cases have produced thorough investigations and prosecutions, as documented in an appendix of case summaries prepared by CPJ's research staff.

As novelist Carlos Fuentes has noted, Mexico "cannot have a true democracy if opposition spokespersons are never presented on television. You have to hear what they have to say. And there are threats against journalists, which sometimes end in death. All these things have to be reformed."

These reforms are beginning to occur, but not without resistance from both the PRI and the press itself. The reports and essays here focus on the transformation of the Mexican press over the past decade, especially in the latter half of the administration of Carlos Salinas de Gortari. The Salinas presidency left many Mexican political and economic institutions radically changed, and the full impact of these changes is only now being felt. We take an especially close look at the role of the Mexican press in the tumultuous final year of the Salinas presidency, 1994, a year of uprisings, elections, assassinations, and economic collapse.

In retrospect, it is clear that 1994 was the year in which the press began to break free of its historic patterns of conformity and control. Many Mexican journalists say they can now write freely about anything or anyone, and the administration of President Ernesto Zedillo appeared just two years later to feel under assault as press accounts aggressively questioned its handling of assassination investigations and economic policies.

Still, much of the Mexican news media remains mired in the self-censoring, synergistic relationship with the ruling party described in the essay that gives this volume its name. It remains difficult to imagine the Mexican press aiming its fire at President Zedillo personally with the tenacity and ferocity that now typifies the national political coverage of much of the South American media. Presidential pronouncements are still carried nearly verbatim on the front pages, with critical commentary confined to a few prominent columnists and the grousing of opposition congressmen. But several leading publishers and broadcasters have discovered that editorial independence is not only possible but often profitable. And that is potentially revolutionary.

There was another motive behind CPJ's interest in this project. Though quintessentially Mexican, the complex interrelationship between the press and the PRI for the past half century has important universal lessons. Much about the government practices and national press culture described in this book will sound familiar to journalists in Bangkok, Buenos Aires and Bratislava. With the replacement of dictatorships of the left and right by nascent democracies around the world, press freedom is unquestionably on the rise. At the same time, pressures on the news media have become more subtle and nuanced. Overt state censorship and state-sponsored violence against journalists are becoming rarer in most regions, but news structures constraining genuine journalistic independence are emerging in their place.

And, as has historically been the case in Mexico, the press is often as much an accomplice as a victim in this new political relationship. In Moscow, where journalists today are murdered on the job with alarming frequency, independent reporters and editors often say they are more afraid of dependency on government financial favors than they are of physical violence. The story of the Mexican press under the PRI is an object lesson in these self-perpetuating cycles of interdependence and intimidation.

Mexico and CPJ's Mission

Mexico had always presented a special challenge to the Committee to Protect Journalists. When CPJ was founded by a group of U.S. foreign correspondents in 1981, the most dangerous place in the world for journalists was Latin America. Scores of reporters, editors and broadcasters had been kidnapped and murdered in Central America and the Southern Cone, most by military death squads. Mexico, while hardly a paragon of democracy, seemed comparatively benign. Indeed, Mexico became a safe haven to many exiled journalists from Argentina, Chile, Guatemala and El Salvador. Mexico's hundreds of daily newspapers spanned a broad ideological gamut and offered extensive national and international news coverage.

Its many journals of opinion were often scathingly critical of government officials and policies, from the perspectives of the radical left, the hard right, and almost everything in between. That this criticism was rarely, if ever, directed at the president himself was hardly abnormal in Latin America, where few leaders of that era tolerated unfriendly scrutiny. The slavishly pro-government slant of television news was also more the regional rule than the exception.

There were direct, egregious government assaults on journalists and press freedom in Mexico: the suspension of state-monopoly newsprint deliveries to unfriendly dailies, the police-orchestrated murder of a prominent political columnist, the brazen use of presidential funds and influence to seize editorial control of an ostensibly independent newspaper. But they were comparatively rare. Violent and even fatal attacks on journalists were becoming more common, especially outside the major cities, but most of these incidents were apparent Colombian-style criminal reprisals for drug-trafficking reporting, as opposed to the ideologically motivated persecution of journalists then typical of the countries immediately south of Mexico.

But much of the rest of Latin America moved on, and Mexico seemingly did not. The government's failure to investigate and prosecute drug-related killings of reporters began to suggest not just cowardice or incompetence, but complicity. And the reluctance of the Mexican press to probe deeply into high-level corruption stood in stark contrast to South America's increasingly aggressive news media, which was toppling presidencies in Brazil and Venezuela.

As the rest of Latin America became gradually more democratic, Mexico seemed mired in its corporatist past. And an integral aspect of that entrenched corporatist culture was the willing participation of many, if not most, leading publishers and editors. It was a marriage of convenience in a system that had little tolerance for divorce. This represented a predicament for press freedom advocates outside and within Mexico: What is the proper response when a key constraint on journalistic independence is the news media itself?

The Mexican press had not always been so submissive. In the late nineteenth century, many Mexican newspapers were the voices of liberal reform, railing against suffocating clericalism and entrenched oligarchies. In the waning days of the Porfirio Díaz dictatorship, Mexican dailies trumpeted the democratic reform appeals of Francisco Madero and the land-claim demands of Emiliano Zapata. But in the decade following the 1910-1920 Revolution, as the new regime consolidated its single-party corporatist rule, the Mexican press again became one of the many sectors dependent on and subservient to the government. Financial incentives, official intimidation and genuine loyalties to the new post-Revolutionary state all contributed to this peculiarly Mexican formula of ideological diversity and political dialogue and dissent operating within unmarked but universally understood boundaries.

Some newspapers became the willing servants of factions within the ruling circle: labor unions, industrialists, civil servants, party-line intellectuals. With subsidized newsprint, state control of newsstand distribution, circulations inflated by government purchasing and advertising revenues dependent on government advertising and a revolving-door relationship between newspaper editors and government press offices, there was little opportunity or incentive to develop a genuinely independent national news media.

Press freedom problems in Mexico are still rooted in this historic symbiosis. A complex mix of coercion, conviction, blandishment and fear continues to keep most Mexican press coverage favorable to the interests of the president and the ruling party. The consequences for big-city publishers who break free of this pattern are no longer terribly onerous, providing that their newspapers are potentially self-sustaining enterprises. But for many publications, reliant as they are on government cash, a declaration of independence would be tantamount to a declaration of bankruptcy.

This is the system that President Carlos Salinas de Gortari was once expected to end. But he left the essence of it intact. This was due either to an uncharacteristic failure of political nerve or to his assessment that the advantages of a subservient media outweighed the systemic risks of continuing corruption and skewed information. Salinas's priority was economic reform, not democratization.

In 1988, in a conversation with foreign reporters, the chief press aide to then-candidate Salinas volunteered his view that the Mexican press itself had become an obstacle to his boss's quest for the country's "modernization." He acknowledged that much of the Mexican press was propped up by subsidies, some direct, some clandestine, offered in tacit exchange for immunity from real scrutiny and a guarantee of good play and minimal editorial intervention for the party's message of the day or year. Among the many problems with this arrangement, when viewed from within the Salinas campaign, was the law of diminishing returns. A sold-out press over time loses credibility and hence its effectiveness as an instrument of political control. In becoming utterly unreliable as a source of factual information, the press was failing to meet another basic need of politicians, policymakers and business leaders.

A freer and more professional press, members of the Salinas team contended, would better serve the interests of its economic reform program — especially since the incoming administration was supremely confident of its capacity to use modern media campaigns to sell its plans for privatization and growth to middle-class voters. The archaic, almost slavish dependence on government financial favors and news handouts of most Mexican news organizations had become a perceived handicap for the Salinas presidential campaign, which was unable to connect with a disaffected electorate.

Then why not do something about it? As President Miguel de la Madrid's heir-designate, Salinas already exercised tremendous sway over government institutions. And the presidential campaign was by far the biggest priority and beneficiary of the vast system of media subsidies and controls. If the system was dysfunctional as well as corrupting and expensive, why not do away with it?

Can't do it, the aide said: bad timing. "Elections," he said, "are never the opportune moment to try these things."

In 1988, the traditional structures of Mexican press controls were still largely in place. Coercion was less important than collusion: publishers had become rich as ruling party money insulated them from the realities of the marketplace. Bribery was an institutionalized aspect of the political reporter's trade. Presidential elections were the most lucrative beat of all: it was a standing joke how the campaign press corps became ever more elegantly attired as the campaign progressed. Salaries were a minor part of some reporters' incomes. Official campaign funds also subsidized newspapers directly, paying handsomely for front-page reprints of speeches and press releases masquerading as independently reported news.

In addition, the government held a legal monopoly on the importation and production of newsprint, which it provided to publishers at steep discounts. State industry, which included not just the nationalized oil business but the phone company and the airlines and the entire commercial banking and insurance industries, doled out the lion's share of newspaper advertising, with friendly publications receiving disproportionate patronage at inflated rates. Television news, the biggest single beneficiary of the government's huge commercial advertising budget, was entirely in the hands of one staunch defender of the single-party state.

And then there was fear. The murder of the country's best-known political columnist four years earlier remained unsolved, the investigation paralyzed and critical evidence destroyed, with ever-clearer indications of direct involvement in both the crime and cover-up at the highest level of the country's security forces. The killing was simply the most notorious of many examples of retribution exacted against reporters who had looked too closely at questionable government contracts, electoral fraud machinations or — the most dangerous topic — the narcotics trade. At least six other prominent journalists had been murdered during De la Madrid's term. In the most recent case, the April 1988 murder of Tijuana columnist Héctor Félix, a son of one of Salinas's ruling-party patrons was a leading suspect. He was assumed, apparently correctly, to be politically untouchable. He was never even questioned by police.

When President Salinas left office in 1994, much had changed. He had ordered his cabinet ministries to end direct cash payments to beat reporters and urged state governments to follow suit. (The practice continued, especially on the local level, but it was at least now officially proscribed.) He ended the state newsprint monopoly, over the fierce objections of publishers who had grown accustomed to below-market prices. By privatizing the government's television network, he helped set up the first evening news competitor to Televisa, the quasi-monopoly national broadcasting empire. In contrast to his predecessors, he conspicuously refrained from using the vast power of the presidency to thwart the establishment of new independent dailies in Mexico City and Guadalajara.

That is not to say Salinas was a born-again press freedom advocate: his aides bullied too-critical editors and publishers and pressured radio broadcasters to cancel call-in shows that gave too much air time to the president's critics. And the owner of Mexico's new television network had won the bid only after guaranteeing that the PRI would not be subjected to genuinely critical or probing news coverage. And we now know that the president's brother Raúl Salinas was a silent partner in the new network — while at the same time investing in businesses with rival Televisa's news anchors. But as coverage of the chaotic events of 1994 proved, by the end of the Salinas presidency, the Mexican government was no longer able to set the parameters of national news reporting.

This historic change was due less to the conscious reforms of a modernizing government than to the inadvertent consequences of economic reform, which coincided with (and helped provoke) increasing strength and sophistication of opposition parties in major states and Mexico City itself. Privatization, deregulation, and the opening to foreign investment all helped make the press more independent. The massive turnover of state industries to a clutch of private business empires made advertising sources more plentiful and diverse, depriving the federal government of much of its centralized power to punish critics and reward friends. The rising U.S. investment stake in Mexico after NAFTA has led to more thorough and aggressive U.S. reporting about Mexico, which has helped spur Mexico's news organizations to become more competitive and independent in their own coverage.

Still, many of the historic problems remained, including both the threat and reality of violence against troublesome reporters and editors.

In 1993, the penultimate year of the Salinas government, five journalists were reported murdered in Mexico, more than in any other country in the Western Hemisphere. However, as is commonly the case in Mexico, it was difficult to demonstrate direct linkage between these deaths and the victims' work as journalists. In several instances circumstantial evidence suggested strongly that the homicides were common crimes committed with no apparent political motive. In no case were the victims known for controversial or critical reporting. Yet the chilling effect on Mexican journalism was nonetheless real. There have been well-documented cases in the past of journalists killed for their reporting with the apparent complicity or even participation of local (and in some cases national) law enforcement authorities. And with the endemic failings of the Mexican criminal justice system, those who order such killings are only rarely apprehended, tried and convicted. As in Colombia, most serious physical attacks on journalists appear to have been ordered by drug traffickers.

In small provincial cities, Mexican reporters have reason to fear reprisals. In the national media, however, the suppression of independent reporting has other systemic causes.

Foreign analysts conventionally ascribe the pro-government slant of most Mexican news reportage to two factors: journalists' fear of personal (and often violent) retribution and state control of newsprint supplies and advertising budgets. Few Mexican reporters share that analysis, however, as Raymundo Riva Palacio and other contributors to this book stress. Direct physical intimidation of journalists is less frequent than it was in the past. Privatization and deregulation have reduced the government's control over advertising revenue. Yet even under Zedillo, the PRI strives to manipulate coverage through political pressure and economic favors to pro-government news organizations. And these favors are all too often willingly received. Despite the many highly honorable exceptions, the Mexican press remains the least independent news media of any major country in the Western Hemisphere.

The central problem is not easily remedied: it is the sycophancy and corruption of the news media itself. There are honorable exceptions, such as the muckraking national newsweekly *Proceso,* founded two decades ago by journalists fleeing the PRI takeover of a leading Mexico City daily; the conservative, highly professional *El Norte* of Monterrey and its three-year-old sister paper, *Reforma* of Mexico City; *El Financiero,* the country's leading business daily; the increasingly independent, left-leaning *La Jornada,* and *Siglo XXI,* a feisty new Guadalajara tabloid; *El Diario de Yucatán,* a starchy defender of regional business interests; and the newsweekly *Zeta* of Tijuana, which survived the assassination of its co-founder to show that investigative journalism can thrive even in the country's most dangerous precincts. The success of these publications has shown that independent reporting in Mexico is not only possible but financially rewarding.

Most publishers, however, preferred the old system of under-the-table government subsidies for their underpaid reporters and over-the-table payments for official "news" placement. President Carlos Salinas de Gortari's dissolution of the state monopoly that provided subsidized newsprint was bitterly opposed by most publishers. His announced ban on cash bribes to reporters from federal offices was received with greater equanimity, since there are multiple alternative mechanisms for such payments.

Independent broadcast reporting is no longer unknown, now that Televisa faces local competition. Radio call-in and interview shows have begun to offer opposition viewpoints, but official complaints have in some cases led the radio companies to cancel the offending programs. Most television news — condemned as "Stalinist" and "an embarrassment" by Fuentes, whose views on the subject are shared by most leading Mexican intellectuals — still hews rigidly to the government line. When Chiapas rebels took arms against the government on the first day of 1994, one of their principal complaints was against "biased" television news reporting. In subsequent negotiations, the government agreed to guarantee fairer television coverage of opposition views and candidates during the 1994 election, an extraordinary admission of how skewed such reporting had been in the past and how the government was able to influence the editorial policy of ostensibly independent broadcasters.

Free Trade, Free Press

There is no question that Mexicans are *entitled* to access to a free press. All citizens of countries that are signatories to the Universal Declaration of Human Rights are guaranteed the right "to seek, receive and impart information through any media and regardless of frontiers." The Mexican Constitution also upholds the principle of press freedom (albeit not without caveats about public order and morality). But as a practical political and economic matter, is there something more than rights and philosophy that makes press freedom a *requirement* for Mexico's overall progress? And, outside Mexico, is there anything inherently significant about this issue, any reason for it to concern anyone other than people with a professional interest in Latin America or journalism?

In the rest of North America, there is one important new reason why freedom of expression and information in Mexico has importance beyond Mexico's borders: the North American Free Trade Agreement. The NAFTA pact makes the entire continent from Chiapas to Alaska one economy with common rules. Press freedom traditions are an integral part of Canadian and American political culture and the foundation for the free exchange of information that has made North American financial markets the most dynamic in the world. The real issue for Mexico is not compliance with the letter or spirit of NAFTA but whether Mexico will be able to compete — and prosper — in an open North American economy without an assertive, pluralistic and fully independent news media. The freedom and vigor of the Mexican press will be a critical test of the NAFTA process and a lesson and precedent for future such accords with other nations and regions.

Put simply: Does free trade require a free press? The answer isn't self-evident. Several successful East Asian economies have combined open commerce with closed political systems. In Singapore, often cited in surveys as one of the most efficient places to do business in the world, journalists who criticize the government or release accurate but unauthorized economic data face heavy fines and jail terms. It's an important question but one that was rarely asked during the long debate over NAFTA.

American and Canadian NAFTA supporters generally accepted the proposition that democratic elections and a free-market economy were preconditions for Mexico's inclusion in a continental free trade zone. This implied that press freedom prevailed in all the three NAFTA countries. Most NAFTA proponents would have agreed that aggressive, independent news reporting is essential to any functioning democracy and a prerequisite for the fair and efficient functioning of free markets.

Yet coverage of the NAFTA debate within Mexico itself was evidence of the limits of press independence there. Dissent was almost inaudible. Outside a few small left-leaning periodicals in Mexico City, there was little questioning of the basic premises of the accord and even less independent reporting on its probable impact on vulnerable sectors of the Mexican population and economy. The tone for most news reports was set by Televisa's uncritical amplification of the government's own pronouncements and its dutiful chronicling of the trilateral negotiations and NAFTA-related presidential campaign debates and congressional battles in the United States. Any troubling Mexican economic news was suppressed by the government or systematically downplayed by most of the Mexican press. The Salinas administration helped subsidize commercial television and daily newspapers with an expensive pro-NAFTA government advertising campaign, while at the same time paying U.S. and Mexican public relations professionals — and sometimes paying journalists and newspapers directly — to get pro-NAFTA stories placed prominently in the press. Throughout the NAFTA negotiation and ratification process, Mexican opinion polls showed strong majority support for the agreement. But this hardly represented the informed consent of the governed.

Business interests seeking to take advantage of Mexico's newly opened markets have a vested interest in press freedom and pluralism, though few seem to recognize it. Tight controls on Mexican government financial data and private sector business information have functioned as de facto constraints on cross-border trade. It is now conventional wisdom that the December 1994 devaluation debacle would have been avoided if the government had been more systematic and forthright in the disclosure of its foreign-reserve and current-account figures. A genuinely independent press would not have allowed the government to treat this ostensibly public information as its own private property, to be disclosed only at a moment and in a manner of its own choosing.

With NAFTA in place, concerns about press freedom are no longer merely a domestic issue. Canadians and Americans now also have a vested interest in the free flow of information across and within all three countries' borders. The North American Free Trade Agreement touches directly on many technical issues involving the flow of news and business information across borders and within each NAFTA nation, including provisions on copyright codes, computer communications, reciprocal investment rights in cable and broadcasting ventures and ownership and distribution rules for print media. This means that many present and potential investors have legitimate business reasons to seek reassurances that a free press in Mexico is not just a constitutionally guaranteed right, but an irreversible political and economic fact.

Yet few U.S. (or Canadian) media conglomerates sought such assurances at the time of NAFTA's negotiations. That's because few seemed aware of the real opportunities for investment and profit in the Spanish-language news business both north and south of the border. Maine potato growers, California software wizards, Missouri broommakers — all weighed in, vigorously and insistently, with their varied parochial concerns about the free trade agreement. Negotiators were bombarded by requests from virtually every industry in the United States for detailed assurances that NAFTA would both oblige their Mexican competitors to forgo subsidies and other distorting state-provided privileges and allow Americans to sell and invest in Mexico on the same terms that Mexican companies are allowed to sell and invest in the United States. In almost every industry under negotiation, American business interests prevailed. The news business was a conspicuous exception.

In a provision that attracted surprisingly little attention at the time, NAFTA lets U.S. investors acquire no more than 49-percent minority equity interest in daily newspapers "written primarily for a Mexican audience and distributed in Mexico." Similarly, it limits U.S. investors to a 49-percent share in Mexican-based newswires, computer information and communication networks and other "videotext services." The only news operations in Mexico where U.S. investors can exercise full equity control are those that simply republish and distribute within Mexico a foreign-edited newspaper or foreign-edited newswire ("videotext") services.

The American news business has several muscular lobbying associations, but all shrugged off the issue of NAFTA and press freedom in Mexico. The National Association of Broadcasters, which represents radio and television news organizations, never took a clear stance on NAFTA in public or private representations to U.S. trade negotiators or congressional committees.

The print media was only slightly more engaged. Just six weeks before the 15-month NAFTA negotiations concluded, the Newspaper Association of America (NAA) sent a seven-paragraph letter to the State Department saying it had "just come to our attention that the United States is about to negotiate a free trade agreement with Mexico that would affect the newspaper publishing business and free press matters negatively." The NAA — the industry's chief lobbying association, representing 1,700 newspapers that account for 90 percent of the country's daily newspaper circulation — complained that the 49-percent limitation would "stifle the dissemination of diverse news and information." The NAA continued: "The unfettered flow of news and information in international commerce depends upon the ability of an independent press to emerge and operate freely in various countries. A free press cannot thrive where government limits ownership of newspaper publishing businesses. It is troubling that the United States government would endorse a policy so antithetical to the free speech and press protections guaranteed in this country by our Constitution."

The NAA was told in reply that its viewpoint would be considered. It wasn't. Mexico's 49-percent limitation was adopted without change, and the U.S. newspaper industry never pursued the matter. The U.S. newspaper industry had no immediate economic interest in Mexico because before NAFTA it wasn't allowed to have such interests. Mexican newspapers, by law and tradition, had always been wholly Mexican-owned. NAFTA, like most foreign trade issues, is a "tangential" matter to the NAA, an executive there noted at the time: "No members asked us to look into it."

It is not only U.S. publishers who have seemed uninterested in press freedom issues south of the border. The influential American Society of Newspaper Editors invited then-President Salinas to be the featured speaker at its 1991 annual meeting and extended the same invitation to President Zedillo at its 1994 meeting. Salinas was lauded by his hosts for ostensibly ensuring that "the newspapers of his country are as free to express their views and opinions as the [U.S. and other foreign] newspapers that he has on his desk every morning." Salinas fielded questions about oil, Florida oranges, the environment, labor rights, and Eastern Europe, among other things, but press freedom issues were never raised by the assembled editors. Nor was Zedillo subjected to such questioning three years later.

Mexican limitations on news media ownership are an anomaly in an agreement that swept away almost all restrictions on U.S. investment in Mexico. The only other major exceptions to NAFTA's liberalizing rules are those where foreign control is expressly prohibited by the Mexican constitution (oil, electricity) or equally restrictive U.S. investment rules (affecting airlines, coastal shipping and broadcasting). The news business — television and radio network ownership aside — fits neither of these categories.

Indeed, the news media are also among the few industries where reciprocity for Mexican investors in the United States is more than an abstract matter. Mexican investors can and do own U.S. periodicals and news services. Mario Vázquez Raña, a Mexican newspaper publisher with close government ties, was for several years the controlling stockholder of United Press International. Emilio Azcárraga, the billionaire owner of Televisa, Mexico's near-monopoly commercial broadcaster, profiled in this volume by Marjorie Miller and Juanita Darling, is the largest U.S. publisher of Spanish-language magazines and the largest provider of Spanish-language television news services to Spanish-speaking Americans. Azcárraga and other Mexican broadcasters also supply news programming to many of the 330 Spanish-language radio stations in the United States.

It is not a level playing field. Under U.S. law, Mexicans may transmit news broadcasts from Mexico aimed primarily at the United States, but Mexican law forbids a U.S. company from broadcasting news programming aimed at a Mexican audience from within the United States. The United States also allows Mexican companies to control U.S. cable networks and provide news programming through those networks. In Mexico, by contrast, NAFTA allows no more than 49-percent U.S. ownership in Mexican cable television networks and in suppliers of programming for cable television in Mexico.

Corruption is an investment problem: if you are a foreign investor in the news business and your wholly owned Mexican competitor is subsidized by under-the-table government payments, this is not only unfair but, under NAFTA, illegal and a legitimate area for inquiry by NAFTA dispute resolution bodies.

This is not just a business issue. In Central European countries that are trying to build new democracies and market economies, such restrictions on outside investment in the news media have been rejected as impediments to the development of truly free and professional press.

Press freedom in Mexico is not just Mexico's affair, then. The NAFTA framework provides an opening to address the issue as a legitimate business concern for the North American news media at large, without the patronizing taint of cross-border moralizing. This interest would be quietly welcomed by the many Mexican news professionals who are trying to compete without favors and without fears.

Zedillo's Turn

President Ernesto Zedillo came into office promising a new era of openness and fairness in official dealings with the news media. But it is a sign of how far Mexico has to go that one of Zedillo's first initiatives was to hold a press conference with Mexico City reporters on Mexico's Press Freedom Day, as if that were in itself a gesture of benevolence.

Most Mexican journalists agree that there is a new mood of independence in the news media, though many attribute this more to the perceived political weakness of the government than to a new official respect for press freedom. Leading newspapers are increasingly aggressive in their reporting and critical on their opinion pages of the PRI and its officials. Televisa's unexpected decision in early 1996 to broadcast a devastating videotape of a massacre of unarmed peasants by Guerrero state police eventually led to the resignation of the PRI governor and was hailed by many observers as a turning point for Mexican television news. Cynics, though, noted that it was in the interest of the Zedillo administration to drive the recalcitrant governor from office. A better test would be if the credibility or integrity of Zedillo loyalists and cabinet ministers is directly challenged by television news reports.

Journalists are still often harassed by state and municipal authorities and by private citizens who appear to enjoy the protection of local politicians and police. Despite the Zedillo government's promise to reform the criminal justice system and to probe further into political assassinations, the murders of three journalists in the small state of Morelos over a six-week period in 1994 did not prompt a serious federal investigative effort. Though the killings took place before Zedillo assumed office, his attorney general declined to treat the crimes as a federal matter.

In its negotiations with opposition parties over election reforms, the Zedillo administration has tacitly acknowledged that television coverage has been skewed in the ruling party's favor. The government pledged to help ensure greater and fairer coverage of antigovernment candidates in television news, an offer welcomed by opposition politicians but criticized by many news professionals as a potential formula for further state intervention in private newsgathering.

Pro-government self-censorship continues to characterize much of the printed press, especially in the provinces. These problems are exacerbated by the endemic corruption in the country's criminal justice system, a problem Zedillo has identified as one of his priorities. Violent assaults against journalists, including homicides, are rarely thoroughly investigated. In too many cases, this failure to enforce the law is clearly due to fears that a serious prosecutorial effort would collide with entrenched local interests. This syndrome is hardly confined to crimes against journalists: this is a criminal justice system that has been incapable of credibly investigating the assassinations of the ruling party's own presidential candidate and congressional majority leader. But Zedillo, like Salinas before him, should demonstrate unambiguously that the government views violent attacks against journalists as attacks against the Constitution's guarantees of press freedom for all Mexicans.

Drug trafficking, as in much of the rest of Latin America, now constitutes the most serious physical threat to journalists in Mexico. In border cities such as Matamoros and Tijuana, and in drug-trafficking centers in the interior such as Sinaloa and Guerrero, narcotics cartels operate with impunity. Journalists who attempt to cover their activities face violent reprisals. Only rarely will the state or federal government offer protection to threatened journalists or aggressively investigate assaults or even murders of journalists that appear to be connected to drug trafficking. One disturbing example: accused drug cartel kingpin Juan García Abrego was turned over by the Zedillo government to U.S. prosecutors for murders he had allegedly ordered in the United States, even though García Abrego is also said to have ordered the 1986 murder of a leading editor in the border town of Matamoros.

Despite these chronic problems, the Mexican news media are changing. The best Mexican newspapers and radio news services today are more professional and openly critical than all but a handful of major news outlets elsewhere in Latin America. Institutional coercion and intimidation of the press has unquestionably abated.

As Mexico heads into its 1997 congressional election, Zedillo's pledges will face their real test. For the first time since its founding, the PRI could conceivably lose control of the Congress. Zedillo will face enormous internal pressure to harness the power of the media on behalf of the interests of the ruling party. Even without Zedillo's support, ruling party powers will use all the traditional levers of coercion and co-optation that remain at their disposal. The July 1997 legislative contest will therefore also be the best measure yet of the independence and integrity of Mexico's press, which no longer has any valid professional excuse for failing to resist these pressures. The risks for the system are enormous: if next year proves to be the beginning of the end of the culture of collusion, it could also signal the imminent demise of the PRI itself.

Section I

The Print Media

Chapter 1

A Culture of Collusion:
THE TIES THAT BIND THE PRESS
AND THE PRI

Raymundo Riva Palacio

Foreigners have long believed that the Mexican government controls the press through the sale of newsprint by a company the government owns.

Are they right?

Wrong.

Foreigners have long believed that the Mexican government exercises an overwhelming power to suppress or publicize any news or opinion it wants.

Are they right?

Again, wrong.

Conclusion: There is a free press and freedom of expression in Mexico.

Right?

Once more, wrong.

Raymundo Riva Palacio has been an investigative reporter, foreign correspondent, foreign editor and opinion columnist for several major Mexican publications, including Excélsior *and* El Financiero. *He also served as director of the official government news agency, Notimex. Currently he is a columnist and head of the investigative reporting team of the Mexico City newspaper* Reforma. *He completed a research project on the Mexican media while serving as a Nieman Fellow at Harvard University from 1991 to 1992. His most recent book is* Beyond the Limits *(1995), a textbook for journalism students.*

The Mexican press censors itself. Outside observers who look for examples of direct government censorship, monopolization of the distribution of newsprint and limitless government power to suppress or publicize news and commentary fail to grasp the nature of the relationship between the government and the media — a complex network of mutual benefits, commitments and favors, difficult to penetrate and even more difficult to reform. In general, the collusion of the press is so complete that the government does not even have to resort to direct censorship to suppress ideas and information. The government is the country's largest advertiser. Nearly 250 newspapers throughout Mexico derive most of their income from advertising paid for by the government. A newspaper with a large staff but small circulation need not concern itself with selling newspapers since it can live almost entirely on government advertising. Take, for example, the case of one national newspaper in Mexico City. In the first year of Carlos Salinas de Gortari's administration, it had a circulation of only 5,000, but it thrived from government advertising and boasted of a staff of more than 250 and first-quarter profits of nearly US$1 million.

The government and many politicians buy space in the form of news bulletins promoting their activities or simply reprinting speeches. Of course, the newspapers never inform their readers that they are reading paid advertising rather than hard news. Politicians from the ruling party can buy almost any amount of news space they want.

Since they lack readership and private-sector advertising, most newspapers and magazines could not continue to publish if the government withdrew its paid advertising. According to figures given in the *1990 Directory of Mexican Media*, the combined daily circulation of Mexico City's 25 newspapers was 2,916,625 copies. In 1990, investigative journalist Raúl Trejo Delarbre, in a supplement to the magazine *Nexos*, estimated that the correct circulation figure was closer to 731,000 copies per day.[1] Both figures include sports publications and sex scandal sheets, which in both surveys accounted for nearly half of all papers sold. According to Trejo Delarbre, the combined editions of the nine major newspapers published in Mexico City in 1990 — *El Día, Excélsior, El Financiero, El Heraldo, La Jornada, Novedades, El Sol de México, El Universal* and *unosmásuno* — totaled no more than 282,000 copies. This is just 4,000 more than the 278,000 1990 daily circulation of the *San Jose Mercury News* of California, then the 36th-largest newspaper in the United States.[2] According to a confidential report by the Mexican government, the combined circulation of the same nine papers was estimated at 550,315, or 12,000 fewer than the *San Francisco Chronicle*, then the ninth most widely circulated paper in the United States.[3]

There are no official auditors to supply reliable circulation numbers; inevitably, the numbers offered by the publications themselves are dubious,

Moreover, advertising agencies place no pressure on the media to provide accurate figures. Since circulation is not considered important, newspapers neither compete for readers nor form public opinion independently. Instead, they aid the government in forming political opinion, playing a role that both the press and the government acknowledge and accept. Government money keeps them in business, and there is no need to rely on private-sector advertising — even though this arrangement leaves newspapers and journalists extremely vulnerable to government coercion and blackmail.

Government officials can threaten to withdraw paid stories and inserts if a newspaper or journalist refuses to publish a particular story or, more commonly, refuses to suppress certain facts. In the early 1980s, President José López Portillo ended all paid contributions to *Proceso* and *Crítica Política* because they criticized his policies. *Proceso* managed to survive on commercial advertising, but *Crítica Política* did not. President Miguel de la Madrid withdrew the government's paid inserts to *El Financiero* because officials disagreed with its coverage of foreign debt negotiations. *El Financiero* stayed afloat with private-sector advertising.

The vast majority of news magazines, newspapers and journals would disappear if the government were to subject the press to the same free-market policies that have had such widespread impact on other sectors of the economy. However, "survival of the fittest" among newspapers would radically change the relationship between the government and the press. Financially independent newspapers could finally criticize the government with impunity.

Perks, Kickbacks and Concealed Weapons

Only a handful of news organizations in Mexico operate independently; most editors and reporters toe the official line. In the newsroom, reporters compete with each other for the richest beats — rich not in terms of information but in political advertising — because this is the main source of their income. Reporters seek out government "news" reports to earn commissions for their "stories."

Elsewhere, the practice of awarding advertising commissions to reporters would provoke charges of conflict of interest and unethical journalism. Since the concept of conflict of interest doesn't exist in Mexican journalism, this widespread practice is not seen as unethical. Indeed, many journalists think of it as a legal way to increase their incomes, since no law prohibits them from receiving commissions.

Officials also promote the payment of bonuses to journalists. The most common form is the kickback, known as the *embute* or *chayote* in the jargon of Mexican journalism. The *embute* is generally handed to journalists in a sealed envelope and is referred to by the press and politicians alike as "help" to improve journalists' salaries.[4] Kickbacks may be handed out on a monthly basis to beat reporters or during official tours. The amount varies according to the beat, the reporter and the news organization. It can be as low as $20 or as high as $2,000 per month.

One presidential aide used to boast that the Salinas administration no longer gave money to journalists. Technically, he was right. However, employees at the presidential press office asked politicians to contribute money to journalists who accompanied the president on trips. During one trip to the state of Nayarit in the summer of 1990, for example, a local politician sponsored a banquet for 300 people and made prostitutes available to any journalists who requested them, according to reporters who were there. During Salinas' presidential campaign, the Institutional Revolutionary Party (Partido Revolucionario Institucional — PRI) press team rented nightclubs for journalists. Until fairly recently, journalists traveled free with the president and government officials on government airplanes or on commercial flights paid for by the government. They stayed in five-star hotels and enjoyed free meals and telephone lines to any part of the world. It is difficult to believe that Salinas was not aware of the benefits journalists enjoyed. At best, high-ranking government officials willingly close their eyes to what goes on.

In several cases, editors and publishers have fired reporters after it became public knowledge that they had accepted kickbacks or "contributions." In general, however, editors allow reporters to take kickbacks to compensate for low salaries.

Since the federal budget for press and propaganda is not publicized, no one can say with absolute certainty how much money the government funnels into paid news stories and kickbacks to journalists. But it is enough to keep shoddy journalism in business. Politicians also have access to funds that are not under any kind of administrative control. They often go so far as to give favored journalists the latest model car or perhaps a paid vacation in Europe for the entire family. The former governor of Chiapas, Gen. Absalón González, once paid an editor $40,000 to have a negative article about him pulled from the paper. In another case, a top official in the Ministry of Communication received an eight-column banner headline on the front page of a major newspaper in exchange for a telephone line. In 1992, Televisa's public relations representative sent reporters televisions, VCRs and home videos for Christmas. A number of private companies, following the government's lead, pay journalists for space to promote their products under the guise of news articles.

Without resigning from their jobs as journalists, some editors and reporters also work for politicians as public relations consultants. Other forms of the government's deal with the press are endless. During the Salinas administration, a former attorney general for Mexico City decided to stop giving cash to journalists. Instead, his office enabled journalists to be paid for helping free certain criminals from jail. Although the help was restricted to those convicted of minor offenses, the former official's staff provided that service twice a month, allowing the journalists to charge the families of prisoners for "services" rendered.

The Ambivalence of Reform

S hortly after Carlos Salinas de Gortari was nominated for the presidency by the PRI in October 1987, one of his press advisers euphorically announced that radical changes in the government's relations with the press were waiting in the wings. But radical change never came. Salinas intensified the economic reforms initiated by his predecessor, confronting the business world, manufacturers, trade unions, drug traffickers and tax evaders. However, neither Salinas nor his administration confronted the press. The Unión de Voceadores de México, which controls the direct distribution of newspapers and magazines in Mexico City, remained intact.

Perhaps Salinas avoided extending his reforms to the press because he feared that an angry press might provide space for his political enemies. The 1988 electoral contest had been a particularly bitter fight, and rifts within the PRI had weakened Salinas' presidency. Or perhaps radical changes in government-press relations could only take place in the context of profound political reform — something Salinas was neither ready nor inclined to carry out.

In any case, the press continued to serve the purposes of the Salinas administration. Television and radio were subject to a licensing system by which the government had the right to revoke licenses or refuse their renewal at its discretion. Control of the written press was far more subtle. While radio and television carried messages for popular consumption, the print media, especially the political columns of Mexico City's major newspapers, communicated primarily with the elites.

For its part, the press remained equally committed to the status quo. In July 1989, when President Salinas first proposed liquidating the state-owned Productora e Importadora de Papel, S.A. (PIPSA), the country's largest distributor of newsprint, publishers and editors from various newspapers asked him to reconsider. While the commonly held belief that the Mexican government exercises strict control over the press through the sale and distribution of newsprint is exaggerated, PIPSA did refuse in 1976 to supply newsprint to *Proceso*, a new publication at that time. The publishers had to borrow paper from other magazines or buy it on the black market. The media's response to the government's initiative to privatize PIPSA was not surprising. Among other things, they argued that the publishing sector would suffer considerably if abandoned to the free market. President Salinas decided against closing PIPSA but eliminated its monopoly and abolished restrictions that prevented individual publishing companies from importing their own newsprint.

During its first year, the Salinas administration also floated a proposal to establish an independent auditing institute to verify press circulation figures. Only three newspapers demonstrated any interest. The vast majority side-stepped calls to cooperate, undermining the proposed reform at the outset.

The Salinas administration officially maintained that corruption could be eliminated and journalistic standards raised through presidential orders. In 1992, the government announced it would no longer shoulder media expenses on national and international presidential trips, would reduce its press and advertising budget by 50 percent and would require government agencies to provide receipts for all money given to journalists. These reforms were slated to become law in the spring of 1993 but were never fully implemented, mainly because of a lack of consensus within the Salinas cabinet. Many important government officials were loath to give up their unlimited press and advertising resources at a time of increasing competition from opposition parties.

The administration did meet one long-standing demand of reform-minded journalists by establishing a professional wage for media employees. Unfortunately, this measure did not accomplish its main objective: an overall increase in salaries. Nor did it bring about a general improvement in journalistic standards.

In the fall of 1993, in the state of Veracruz (where the governor was a member of President Salinas' inner circle), state officials orchestrated an attack on opposition presidential candidate Cuauhtémoc Cárdenas by a group of transvestites at a public gathering. The event was recorded on video, and copies were distributed to the Mexican and foreign press. When seen out of context, the clip made it look as if Cárdenas had welcomed the transvestites. An aide to the governor paid for still photos to be prominently displayed in two Mexico City newspapers. Cárdenas also had been invited to deliver the closing speech at a forum organized by the Mexico City daily *Excélsior*. The day before the forum, however, the invitation was withdrawn, and Cárdenas was told that the government had pressured the organizers to cancel his participation.

The Press Revolution That Wasn't

In the early hours of 1994, guerrilla columns of the Zapatista National Liberation Front (Ejército Zapatista de Liberación Nacional — EZLN) marched into and captured five towns in the southern state of Chiapas. This was the first armed movement of the post-Cold War era and the most important uprising in Mexico since the revolution that exploded in 1910.

Nearly three months later, the Mexican regime was hit by still another shock: the assassination of Luis Donaldo Colosio, the official party's presidential candidate. As Colosio was a candidate for the presidency, his death could well be compared to the assassination of Robert F. Kennedy. Its impact on Mexican society, however, was closer to the impact the assassination of President John F. Kennedy had in the United States. The political climate in Mexico became more and more tense as society was hurled into a limbo of fear and uncertainty.

The press was as confused as the rest of the country. Mexican journalists had covered similar events in other countries, but they were overwhelmed by the enormity of these unprecedented events at home. They could not keep their feelings out of their stories and often produced biased and contradictory opinion pieces. Yet the perception emerged — and was filtered through the foreign press — that somehow 1994 was the year the Mexican press finally managed to break free of its dependency on the government and that somehow it was becoming more critical and independent than at any time during the century. This simply was not the case, however.

With few exceptions, the Mexican press remains as financially dependent on the government as it was at the end of 1993. The war in Chiapas, the Colosio assassination and other dramatic events of 1994 did nothing to change the government's policy of disseminating advertising disguised as news stories (*gacetillas*). Nor did it open up channels to information; these remain as airtight and exclusive as ever.

During the war in Chiapas, the Mexican government tried to control information at the source by restricting the press's movements in the conflict zone, not an unusual procedure in wartime. However, restrictions did not apply equally to all media: those who were considered allies or friends, such as Televisa, were not only able to move about in areas under military control but also had military vehicles and helicopters at their disposal. Their reports reflected the official version of the conflict, totally sidestepping that of the rebel forces. A segment of the Mexican press deserves recognition for helping to stop the escalation of the war by adamantly insisting on a negotiated settlement, but the independent press was in the minority. Only a few isolated journalists in Mexico City — the epicenter of decisionmaking — joined in opposing a military solution.

The dramatic events of 1994 simply demonstrated the major flaws of Mexican journalism: lack of ability to develop a story, lack of direction given to young journalists and lack of journalistic technique. When journalists actually reported what was happening, there were no major problems with their work. By simply describing what they saw, they fulfilled their obligations. Their problem was making sense of what they saw.

During the Chiapas war, Mexico City journalists were held hostage by their own shortcomings. Accustomed to reporting declarations instead of facts, they turned every statement into a news story. Rhetoric flourished. Reporters quoted anyone and everyone without bothering to determine who was a reliable, authoritative source. Everyone in Mexico was caught up in the war, but many of the young journalists sent to cover it simply went overboard. Anxious to make a name for themselves, they were not only intrepid but irresponsible. In their quest for exclusive stories, they neglected to check the facts. For example, one day a major Mexico City daily reported in its lead story that fighting had broken out near the Chiapas state capital. If this had been true, it would have meant a serious escalation in the conflict. But it wasn't true. The reporter had confused an assault in a store, where one person was killed and the assailant captured after a struggle, with a military battle. The newspaper never published a correction.

During the war, the lack of editors at most Mexico City papers also took its toll. Often the same edition of a newspaper contained several stories on the same topic with contradictory information. Information was often fragmented and lacked context. This is not unusual for the Mexican press, but at this time the negative consequences were even more serious.

The press did favor the guerrillas — sometimes indirectly, sometimes openly. Undoubtedly, the government's overreaction and complete news blockage influenced the press. Another factor was the surprising press savvy displayed by the Zapatistas, whose seduction of the press merits further study. The anti-government sentiment that exists among many Mexican reporters, as opposed to the pro-government sentiment of the majority of their publishers, certainly played a role, as did an inclination to support the underdog that is deeply embedded in Mexican culture. However, siding with the guerrillas did not constitute responsible, critical reporting.

The same structural defects that plagued the press during the war in Chiapas were also evident in the reporting of the Colosio assassination. On this occasion, the press performed even more poorly because no one provided an easily accessible alternative to the government line, as Subcomandante Marcos had done in Chiapas.

Information was published without placing it in context and without fact-checking. Some facts and details in the cavalcade of items published about the assassination were verified, but many were not. Inevitably, readers became even more confused. Once again, the press failed to distinguish among its sources. Conspiracy theories multiplied, in part because of the government's long-standing practice of using political columnists to pass veiled messages to the elites. Like the rest of the society, the press has been drowning in confusion, unable to recover from its shock and enlighten a public in desperate need of direction.

Is There a Way Out?

One could easily draw an analogy between the American press a century ago and the Mexican press today. The two share many characteristics and deficiencies. Structural problems, ranging from limited information and lack of training to the poor use of resources and isolationism, have held back the Mexican press. Most publishers and editors were trained in the old school of journalism, in which statements weigh more heavily than actions and rhetoric is more important than information. Newspapers are full of speeches, statements and press releases. It is not unusual to read comments from a single source — an invitation to massive disinformation — on topics as varied as health, foreign policy and science.

Mexican newspapers lag behind those in many other parts of the world. The Mexican government does not confront a critical press, not because it is more determined to silence criticism than other governments, but because it has been so successful with subtle measures. The government can exercise control over what it wants published because the press has no desire to give up its share of the bargain; the press cannot bear the idea of unbridled competition.

There are some encouraging signs. Society has changed. The people are better educated and informed. They are in instant contact with the rest of the world through television satellites. The communications revolution has created a society that is more skeptical, more belligerent and more aware of how people live outside Mexico. More and more publishers, editors and reporters reject the current relationship with the government. Rank-and-file journalists are pressuring for change from inside newsrooms. A generational change is under way. Increasingly, better-educated reporters have a different vision of journalism. Difficult questions still remain: How long will it take for change to take place? How profound are the changes the communications revolution will bring?

The future is catching up with the media in other ways. Economic reforms implemented by the Salinas administration already are influencing the media. Privatization and the opening of Mexico's borders to the global economy will also affect the press. Private advertisers will at last be forced to conduct accurate market research. The infusion of foreign capital, the impact of foreign competition and the formation of strategic alliances between Mexican and foreign-owned media companies have already had an impact on print media. *Excélsior* has begun publishing a weekly supplement in English and Spanish for distribution mainly in Texas. *El Financiero* has begun publishing a Saturday and Sunday edition, has created new specialized supplements and has set up a news agency that specializes in information for investors, stock exchanges, banks and brokerage firms. The general director of *El Universal,* Juan Francisco Ealy Ortíz, was invited to join the board of Multivisión, currently Televisa's principal cable network competitor.

Many newspapers are talking with foreign corporations to study possible forms of cooperation and investment, and others have already explored innovative marketing techniques, such as the bilingual supplement covering the North American Free Trade Agreement (NAFTA) jointly published by *El Imparcial* of Hermosillo and the *Arizona Republic* of Phoenix. Although the highly publicized joint venture between Dow Jones and *El Norte* for the publication of a general interest newspaper in Mexico City never materialized, the long-standing association between the two news organizations has resulted in an exchange of news stories on a regular basis.

Clearly, economic reform has a momentum of its own. But is it enough? If the government were serious about abolishing an ingrained culture of favors and kickbacks, it would simply stop paying kickbacks, stop paying for indirect subsidies and tax breaks and stop paying for political advertising in the form of "news" bulletins. Such reforms in government-press relations would not only affect the central government but would also have an impact at the state level.

Will the government allow a free press as a rule and not as an exception? If it did, most of the newspapers and magazines currently publishing in Mexico would disappear.

Press reform could inevitably cause a change in the balance of power. The newspapers that survive the initial crisis would begin a fierce struggle in the marketplace. Journalistic quality would improve. Top officials would no longer be able to manipulate the press, and the press would begin to fulfill one of the responsibilities of a free press: it would serve as a check on government performance and power.

Unfortunately, I cannot see that happening in the near future. Instead, I believe that the majority of news organizations — those that fear competition in a free and independent market — will prevail. In all likelihood, the press will be the last institution in Mexico to undergo the process of democratization.

Notes

1. Raúl Trejo Delarbre, 1990, "Periódicos: ¿quién tira la primera cifra?" *Cuadernos de Nexos, Nexos* (June): 1.

2. According to Trejo Delarbre, the circulation figures are as follow:

	Newspaper	Reported	Actual
1.	*La Afición*	98,500	12,000
2.	*Cine Mundial*	50,000	4,000
3.	*Cuestión*	60,000	2,000
4.	*El Día*	n.a.	7,000
5.	*Diario de México*	63,000	4,000
6.	*El Economista*	35,000	4,000
7.	*Esto*	400,200	90,000
8.	*Excélsior*	200,000	90,000
9.	*El Financiero*	100,000	25,000
10.	*El Heraldo de México*	209,000	15,000
11.	*La Jornada*	75,000	40,000
12.	*El Nacional*	120,000	69,000
13.	*The News*	35,000	5,000
14.	*Novedades*	210,000	10,000
15.	*Ovaciones* (morn)	205,000	40,000
16.	*Ovaciones* (aftern)	220,000	80,000
17.	*La Prensa*	300,000	100,000
18.	*El Sol* (morn)	90,000	3,000
19.	*El Sol* (aftern)	92,250	5,000
20.	*Tribuna*	n.a.	4,000
21.	*Ultimas Noticias* (morn)	54,000	25,000
22.	*Ultimas Noticias* (aftern)	54,000	30,000
23.	*El Universal* (morn)	181,375	65,000
24.	*El Universal* (aftern)	85,000	2,000
25.	*unomásuno*	90,000	20,000

According to my own sources, major newspapers' circulation figures are

1.	*El Universal*	85,000
2.	*Excélsior*	78,000
3.	*El Financiero*	70,000
4.	*La Jornada*	45,000
5.	*El Heraldo*	10,000
6.	*unomásuno*	8,000
7.	*Novedades*	6,000
8.	*El Sol* (morn)	5,000
9.	*El Día*	2,000

3. A confidential list used by the government cites the following circulation figures:

	Newspaper	Estimated	Reported
1.	*Excélsior*	86,061	200,000
2.	*Novedades*	66,849	215,714
3.	*El Universal*	154,495	139,797
4.	*El Heraldo*	53,483	—
5.	*unomásuno*	29,522	90,000
6.	*El Sol*	31,981	—
7.	*El Día*	16,847	—
8.	*El Financiero*	47,417	135,000
9.	*La Jornada*	63,660	75,000

4. Until minimum-wage standards were established for journalists in January 1992, 90 percent of Mexican reporters earned between US$100 and US$500 per month. The new minimum-wage standard in Mexico City is 40,000 pesos per day, or US$13.33.

Chapter 2

Trial by Fire:
The Chiapas Revolt,
the Colosio Assassination and the
Mexican Press in 1994

Sergio Sarmiento

M exican journalism is at a point of transition. On the one hand, past restrictions gradually are being lowered. Today the Mexican press is freer than ever. On the other hand, journalists face different kinds of pressures, particularly outside Mexico City. Moreover, there are still cases of journalists who have been subjected to physical abuse and even murdered as a result of their professional activities.

Recently, a series of dramatic events — the Zapatista National Liberation Front (Ejército Zapatista de Liberación Nacional — EZLN) rebellion in Chiapas, the assassination of Luis Donaldo Colosio and the most complex, open electoral campaign in the nation's history — proved to be a trial by fire for Mexican journalists. In covering these events, the media — especially radio and the written press — have demonstrated a degree of independence that has taken everyone by surprise. Nevertheless, greater press freedom has not always been indicative of a more professional press. Increasingly, the Mexican press has not been content to report events but has insisted on taking sides.

Sergio Sarmiento is a columnist for the Mexico City newspaper Reforma. *In July 1995, he was appointed vice president for news operations at Televisión Azteca, Mexico's second-largest television network. He is also a frequent contributor to* The Wall Street Journal *and other U.S. publications, a columnist for Mexican newspapers and a commentator on economics and finance for Mexican broadcast media.*

The Struggle for Independence

The Mexican media have come a long way since those fateful days in 1968 when Mexico City's Paseo de la Reforma resounded with shouts of "prensa vendida" (sold-out press), as student demonstrators marched by the old *Excélsior* building. With few exceptions, both print and broadcast coverage of the student movement was disgraceful. Ironically, in that same year, the appointment of Julio Scherer as editor of *Excélsior*, then the most influential paper in the country, gradually opened the way for a more independent press. Scherer recruited newspaper columnists and reporters who, for the first time, were willing to question the government. In Monterrey, the newspaper *El Norte*, owned by the Junco family, displayed the same vocation for independence.

Nevertheless, it was not always easy to remain independent. In 1975, a group with close ties to President Luis Echeverría ousted Scherer and his group from the management of *Excélsior*. That same year, the government organized a newsprint boycott against *El Norte*. But, despite numerous sacrifices the paper was forced to make, it managed to survive and prosper. The evolution of the independent press could no longer be stopped.

The journalists expelled from *Excélsior* founded new publications, such as the weekly *Proceso* (published by Julio Scherer), the newspaper *unomásuno* (edited at first by Manuel Becerra Acosta) and the intellectual monthly magazine *Vuelta* (published by the poet Octavio Paz). All these publications helped open up the press. They were later followed by *El Financiero*, founded by Rogelio Cárdenas, and *La Jornada*, founded by a group of journalists who left *unomásuno* because of differences over management and news policy.

By the early 1980s, these publications had proved their independence. In fact, even more traditional newspapers, such as *El Universal*, aimed at the lower middle class, and *Excélsior*, were noticeably more independent. Newspapers that refused to change with the times, such as *Novedades*, *El Heraldo de México* and *El Sol de México*, rapidly lost readership and influence.

In 1985, radio news came of age, in direct contrast to Mexican television, which remained excessively subservient to the government. That same year, a series of violent earthquakes rocked Mexico City. For several days to follow, the areas most affected by the earthquakes were without electricity. Battery-operated radios became the only reliable source of instant, independent information during that time. Ever since, radio has enjoyed greater credibility than television.

"Monitor," the Radio Red news program conducted by José Gutiérrez Vivó, opened the door for a combative, if somewhat sensationalist, style of journalism. In Mexico City, millions now turn to radio — once considered merely an entertainment medium — as their principal source of news. "Para

Empezar" (To Begin With), conducted by Pedro Ferriz de Con, brought news programming to FM stations and an audience with greater socioeconomic power. Although its share of the Mexico City market was limited, the show was successful enough to launch a chain of radio stations, enabling "Para Empezar" to reach listeners throughout the country.

Soon, other chains and independent radio stations began to adopt news formats. In the early 1980s, news was a relatively insignificant part of radio programming. By the beginning of the 1990s, however, news programs dominated AM radio and made significant inroads in FM programming. All the major broadcast groups in Mexico produced news programs; competition was intense.

A series of gas explosions in Guadalajara in April 1992 had the same effect on the nation's second-largest city as the 1985 earthquakes had on the capital. *Siglo 21,* a newspaper founded less than a year before the explosions, showed it was not afraid to confront major state and municipal authorities. At the end of 1993, Alejandro Junco de la Vega, publisher of *El Norte* in Monterrey, launched a new paper in Mexico City, *Reforma.* This new start-up soon earned a reputation for independent coverage; its daily circulation rose to 50,000. In fact, by the beginning of 1994, competition among newspapers and radio stations in the nation's major metropolitan areas had become so intense that there was no thought of turning back. Increasingly, Mexicans demanded a higher quality, more independent press.

War Correspondents

The Zapatista rebellion in Chiapas represented a major challenge to the nation's news institutions. Especially during the early days, when Mexican reporters became war correspondents in their own country, the national press showed it was capable of producing highly professional work.

Much of the initial coverage was highly detailed, courageous, independent and reasonably accurate. Particularly outstanding was the reporting of *La Jornada,* whose circulation rapidly increased, often reaching 130,000 copies daily, a 300-percent increase in circulation; *El Financiero,* whose veteran economic reporter, Francisco Gómez Mata, became a war correspondent in his native Chiapas; and the recently founded *Reforma.*

In San Cristóbal de las Casas, the small daily *El Tiempo* became required reading. Among the weeklies, both *Proceso* and *Epoca* provided good news coverage, although each was influenced by its prevailing ideology — the former, pro-leftist and the latter, pro-government.

This was not an easy time for reporters to embark on a crash course in war correspondence. Ismael Romero of *La Jornada* was wounded by gunfire. A correspondent for the Mexico City radio program "Enfoque" recorded a chilling moment during which a group of journalists were apparently attacked by a military plane. Nevertheless, despite such difficulties, even rookie correspondents managed to report their stories without suffering a single fatality.

In the beginning, even television coverage was relatively responsible. After radio had alerted the nation to the uprising (credit is due the program "Noticentro," broadcast by Radio Centro in Mexico City and the Radio Red stations), Televisa and Televisión Azteca broadcast interviews with the rebels on the first and second days of January before much of the written press was able to respond to the news. In his now-classic article, "Extrañas cortesías" (Strange Acts of Courtesy), the writer Gabriel Zaid noted that never before had Mexican television offered its microphones to a group of rebels who had risen against the government.

This first phase of the conflict, however, was brief. Fifteen days after the war began, the government declared a cease-fire, which gave the press time for analysis and reflection. Newspapers and radio shows suddenly had thousands of instant experts on Chiapas, all of whom attempted to "explain" the Zapatista movement.

Some of the commentary was insightful and profound. Arturo Warman, the government ombudsman for agricultural problems, wrote a wide-ranging series of articles for *La Jornada*, describing the complexity of the land ownership problem in Chiapas and the rest of the country. In the same newspaper, Octavio Paz warned that "many of our intellectuals have chosen the easy way out," that they had chosen to make judgments without bothering to listen first. He pointed out that population growth and other factors should be considered in any discussion of the extent of poverty in the state. In *Reforma*, Federico Reyes Heroles warned against "any simplistic explanation" for what was happening in Chiapas. Writing in the same newspaper, Enrique Krauze tried to distinguish between the traditional complaints of indigenous groups in Chiapas and the influence of liberation theology apparent in the Zapatistas' declarations.

Unfortunately, the more profound reflections were in the minority. Most analysts reduced the conflict to a simple cowboy and Indian movie. The Zapatistas were the heroes, modern Robin Hoods determined to defend the rights of millions of Indians who faced oppression and discrimination. The big ranchers (*latifundistas*), the army, the government and neoliberalism were cast as the villains determined to exterminate the Indians. The foreign media offered the same simplistic explanations. Moreover, they faced the additional problem of having to explain the conflict in 40-second sound bites.

In the second phase of the conflict, reporters caught the ideological virus. *Proceso* and *La Jornada* produced numerous pieces that apparently were designed simply to show the admirable heroism of some of the protagonists and the inexcusable villainy of others. In *Excélsior*, reporter

Martha Anaya wrote a series of excellent ideological feature stories. Jaime Aviles wrote beautifully for *El Financiero*, but his work was less substantial than that of his colleague, Miguel Badillo, one of the few reporters who questioned the conventional wisdom that the lands invaded by the Zapatistas were *latifundios*, large ranches owned by powerful, wealthy landowners.

Correspondents clearly demonstrated their feelings during Subcomandante Marcos' first press conference. After his speech, the journalists sent to cover the peace negotiations burst into applause.

Despite their outright sympathy with the Zapatista cause, some journalists produced truly exceptional work. For example, the interviews with Marcos carried out "somewhere in the Lacandona jungle" by a team of reporters led by Blanche Petrich, were excellent, if flattering to Marcos (Petrich eventually won the National Journalism Award for her work on Chiapas). Epgigmenio Ibarra broke away from the mediocrity of television with excellent reports that Multivisión, a subscription television service, broadcast. Javier Solórzano produced a fine series of reports and interviews from Chiapas that were broadcast on radio by "Para Empezar" and by Multivisión.

Televisa was severely criticized for its Chiapas coverage, which stemmed from the anti-Zapatista commentary of the anchors, particularly Jacobo Zabludovsky, rather than the field reporting. The network scored a coup, however, in covering the release of the former governor of Chiapas, Absalón Castellanos, who had been kidnapped and held hostage by the EZLN. (The Zapatistas had specifically banned Televisa from covering them.) The network's coverage of the peace negotiations was adequate, even if Televisa was one of the few major media outlets that was not granted an interview with Subcomandante Marcos, the media star of the moment.

The Zapatistas initially banned Televisión Azteca, the network privatized by the government in 1993, presumably because one of its reporters had offered to pay for information. Once this "misunderstanding" was cleared up, however, Televisión Azteca not only was allowed to continue covering the story in Chiapas, but it was also granted the highly coveted interview with Marcos.

The foreign press was not so fortunate. Some of the special correspondents flown in to cover the war in Chiapas displayed the same inability to explain the complexity of the situation as they had in other parts of the world. Once they realized that there wasn't enough bloodshed in this "indigenous rebellion," they packed their bags and returned to Bosnia. Some of the correspondents based in Mexico produced better work, but their stories were also noticeably marked by the same simplistic reasoning abundant in the opinion pages of national newspapers. In a *New York Times* article, for example, correspondent Tim Golden described President Salinas as being taken aback by the rude demands shouted at him by indigenous groups tired of his administration. Such meetings between the president and indigenous groups were nothing new. However, neither the transcripts nor the television images of this meeting indicated that it was remarkably different from previous encounters.

In contrast, David Asman of *The Wall Street Journal* obtained an important story — more for what wasn't said than for what was said — when he interviewed Manuel Camacho Solís, the former peace commissioner in Chiapas, who refused to deny his interest in the presidency. The ambiguity expressed by Camacho during the Asman interview would dominate Mexico's political panorama for weeks thereafter.

The World of Politics

For a while it seemed as if Chiapas were the only major news story in 1994, and it never stopped being covered by the media. Then a series of shocking events occurred. Luis Donaldo Colosio was assassinated, important businessmen Alfredo Harp Helu and Angel Losada were kidnapped and an electoral campaign began that broke with the norm. The fact that the final electoral outcome was uncertain revealed Mexico's new political complexity.

In general, the Mexican press was independent in its coverage of these events. But often it displayed a disturbing lack of professionalism. Rafael Segovia, a professor at the Colegio de México, noted that television "continues to be pro-government," radio provides a forum for a wide diversity of public opinion, but the written press "is currently dominated by the opposition." He might have added, "by the opposition of the left."

The tendencies of the press to favor Cuauhtémoc Cárdenas, presidential candidate of the Democratic Revolutionary Party (Partido de la Revolución Democrática — PRD), were demonstrated by an inability to understand the political strength of the conservative candidate, Diego Fernández de Cevallos of the National Action Party (Partido Acción Nacional — PAN). The press simply echoed the opinion frequently voiced by Cárdenas and his sympathizers, that Fernández de Cevallos was just a sidekick to the ruling party and therefore unworthy of attention. The team of reporters who covered the PAN candidate often were openly hostile to him, while the opposite was true of those reporters assigned to travel with Cárdenas.

In general, television networks tried to support the governing party's candidate, but the changing political situation required that they at least temper that support. The two principal networks, Televisa and Televisión Azteca, opened their doors to opposition candidates. Still, their news coverage tended to favor the candidate of the governing party. For example, for several weeks after the assassination of Colosio, Televisa transmitted short, positive segments of the late candidate's speeches at all hours. They were broadcast as an homage to Colosio, but it was obvious that they were also intended to bolster the campaign of his successor, Ernesto Zedillo.

Miguel Basáñez, director of the polling firm MOTI (Market and Opinion Research International of Mexico), confirmed that to a great extent swings in popularity of the various presidential candidates can be traced to the extent of television coverage they received. In April, Cárdenas' popularity surged to 24 percent, the direct result, according to Básañez, of a series of radio and television interviews with the candidate. Fernández de Cevallos' rise in the polls after May 12 was clearly the result of his performance during the televised debate. Zedillo's comeback in early June can be traced to the intensive positive coverage he received during the weeks prior to the poll.

Ideology and Independence

It is apparent from this summary of recent events that the written press and radio have become increasingly independent of the government. However, television, the most powerful communications medium, continues to be noticeably pro-government, despite the advances manifested in the coverage of the Chiapas conflict and the 1994 electoral campaign.

Now the great challenge for the written press is to rid itself of its dependence on ideology. Radio, one of the high points of press freedom in Mexico, also remains subject to pressure from authorities as well as self-censorship on the part of station owners.

Perhaps one of the most important consequences of Mexico's slow but steady path toward increased press freedom has been that today journalists face fewer direct physical threats while freely practicing their profession. Even so, 40 journalists have been killed or have disappeared since the beginning of the Salinas administration in 1988. While it appears that most of them were not killed for work-related reasons, some certainly were killed because unknown authorities or criminals were disturbed by their reporting. In Mexico, we still cannot discount the possibility that journalists might suffer physical harm for doing their jobs.

Chapter 3

La Gacetilla:
HOW ADVERTISING MASQUERADES AS NEWS

Joe Keenan

How do you get a story on the front page of a Mexican newspaper? You buy it. The printing of *gacetillas*, paid political announcements disguised as news stories, is a daily occurrence in all of Mexico's major newspapers. Except for subtle clues, there is nothing to distinguish these paid articles from regular staff-written articles or to indicate to the reader that they are not the work of staff writers. Nevertheless, these articles are the products of a press office, sent through the newspapers' advertising offices and printed in the papers for their monetary — not news — value.

On October 6, 1987, the day after the announcement that Carlos Salinas de Gortari would be the Institutional Revolutionary Party's (Partido Revolucionario Institucional — PRI) candidate for the Mexican presidency, four major Mexico City newspapers ran front-page stories on a speech made by the governor of a northern state in support of the PRI's choice. All four stories were published without a reporter's byline; all four highlighted the same part of the governor's speech. Two of the four, published in competing newspapers, were identical — word for word and comma for comma.

The next day three leading papers in the capital published accounts of a speech by the governor of a southern state in support of the Salinas' candidacy. Again, the attention granted to one of Mexico's state governors seemed excessive, and again the wording of the articles was uncannily similar. Far from coincidental, the publication of these articles was an obvious example of a gacetilla.

Joe Keenan was editor of Mexico Journal, *a weekly English-language news magazine published by the Mexico City daily* La Jornada *from 1987 to 1989. He currently works with an environmental organization in the Yucatán peninsula.*

In the following weeks, countless gacetillas would be printed in the Mexican press. Not all would be declarations of "adhesion" to the PRI candidate: some were from officials who had shared a podium with the candidate and were eager to make the event and connection known; some involved declarations from a government-owned company, trying to discredit a recalcitrant union; others, from another government-owned company, downplayed reports of a significant ecological disaster that had been blamed on the company. The majority, as is usually the case, were from state governors — announcing electoral plans, electoral results or just giving speeches, trying all the while to keep their names and activities in the eye of Mexico's capital-based officialdom.

How prevalent are gacetillas? According to a number of newspaper editors and executives, every major capital daily publishes them frequently. Without access to the accounting books of a newspaper, it is hard to say exactly how often they are published. Even with this information, in fact, it would be hard to judge. The majority of newspapers do not keep separate accounts for gacetillas or "social and political advertising," counting them simply as advertising income. But a safe estimate, based on a review of capital newspapers and interviews with some of their editors, is that every major capital daily publishes on average one fully paid front-page story per day. Numerous other gacetillas, of course, are printed on the inside pages.

Despite their prevalence, gacetillas are hardly familiar — and rarely mentioned — outside political circles and the media industry. The unwritten law in the industry is that competing media do not comment on each other's behavior. "The lion doesn't eat its own flesh," as one editor put it. As a result, the practices of the press are simply not reported. Nor is it financially convenient for knowledge of the practice to seep out, since the ability of the papers to charge more for a gacetilla depends directly on the article being interpreted as a genuine story. Above all, since all papers publish gacetillas and profit handsomely from them, it is in no one's interest in the industry to break ranks.

The financial argument is, in the end, the strongest. Mexico City has over 20 daily newspapers, each one scraping for a piece of the country's biggest advertising pie: government advertising. The sweetest piece of this pie is the gacetilla, which pays on average two to three times the price of commercial advertising and even more for a front-page position. An editor of a Mexico City broadsheet says, "Without [the gacetilla] this city would just have a handful of dailies, probably not more than four or five."

Though a tight lid is kept on the practice as a whole, the publication of gacetillas, like any other business venture, could not survive without reliable information for clients. Thus, gacetilla rates are available for the asking at the major newspapers. Their purchase is treated like any other advertising transaction: a bill is prepared, often by the reporter who covers the *fuente*, or beat, passed along to the advertising office and sent at month's end to the client. So commonplace is the practice that a quarterly trade magazine, *Medios Impresos, Tarifas y Datos,* published by Medios Publicitarios Mexicanos S.A. de C.V., lists each paper's gacetilla prices by page, page-fraction or agate line, alongside the paper's "general rate."

The various prices listed for gacetillas hint at the diverse forms paid announcements can take: different rates apply for the sports, financial and "social" pages; some papers have different prices for ads that are boxed off and ads that are not (one-third costlier). One paper even lists a special price for a "gossip column" insertion.

In their most common form, gacetillas are solicited by a reporter covering a certain beat or are suggested by the press chief at a government agency or government-owned company. The national editor of a mass-circulation daily explains, "A reporter might ask the press people to 'back' him on a certain important story, or the press chief might say to the reporter, 'We'll back you for half a page on this one.'" In these cases, the reporter writes the story without any review from the client; it is understood, though, that the client is to receive full coverage and a prime location in the next day's paper, not to mention a sympathetic rendering of the event in question. The general manager of one daily says, "The basic idea is to make sure a speech or event is not buried back in the film ads." The system of "backing" an article is far from foolproof, however. "There are an awful lot of complaints," the general manager says. "[The client] will call up and say, 'I thought we had an understanding, and you only gave me one lousy little column.'"

To avoid this sort of confusion, or when a reporter is not available to cover an event in, say, a state far from the capital, some press offices prefer simply to prepare a bulletin, specify a space and a page and have it inserted. This system has its drawbacks as well, however, including the publication of identical tracts in different newspapers. Furthermore, these gacetillas generally run without a reporter's byline and in a style that may be different from that of the newspaper in which they are published. This can affect, albeit subtly, the credibility of the insertion.

Gacetillas are by no means strictly government funded. Commercial interests, especially large companies (Mexican and foreign), often use gacetillas to announce the appointment of a new member of the board of directors, the promotion of a top executive or the launching of a new product line. These paid announcements are often accompanied by a photo, typically showing the company's top executives standing in a semicircle or shaking hands with the new arrival.

In some cases, a photograph alone may run as a gacetilla. The society pages of many newspapers, for instance, are full of photos of private cocktail parties, baby showers and weddings. Not all of these photos are paid insertions, but most are. The newspapers that list gacetilla rates for their society pages in *Medios Impresos* also list a surcharge to cover the cost of full-color photos.

From a political standpoint, the most important types of gacetillas are the paid political announcements that pose as the newspaper's own articles. But another kind of paid political insertion, one that in some cases is also treated as a type of advertisement, can be found in some of the capital's leading political columns. In some newspapers, the columnists are professional political analysts with long experience in the field. But in many papers, the columns are lengthy, loosely assembled compendiums of political gossip, accusations and praise concerning major and minor officials in the government, unions, government industries and private business. This scattershot approach is easily explained; individuals and groups are paying to have themselves portrayed favorably or their adversaries denounced. The authors of these columns can change daily without affecting the content, since, according to one editor, "Their job is basically typing in a stack of bulletins that have been passed down to them." One joke refers to these columnists as "cash-register typists," but the image only begins to suggest the lucrative nature of their work: at one point a front-page political "tid-bits" column in one of the nation's top newspapers was said to be earning the paper $50,000 per week.

Not all payments to newspaper staff members are routed through the newspaper company; some are simple payoffs made directly to the columnist or reporter. Similarly, of course, not all clients resort to the institutional framework of gacetillas to get good press or criticize their opponents. The result can be confusion within the newspaper as different departments battle for their cut of the paid article. A former publicity director at a Mexico City broadsheet says, "We used to follow the reporters around saying, 'Hey where's the insertion order for the gacetilla?' And they'd say, 'Gacetilla? That wasn't a gacetilla, that was my *article*.' But the same 'article' would have come out in all the other papers."

The problem of keeping payments for specific articles within the company's administrative apparatus is a complicated one, but one that can generally be controlled by a competent editor. The national editor at a mass circulation daily says, "We've never had that problem here. If the editor suspects the article 'has a tail' [was paid for outside the normal channels], he can simply leave it out. The reporter then comes in and asks why his article didn't run, and the editor gives a little smile and says there wasn't enough space. It's a way of disciplining the reporters."

Publishing gacetillas can cause other conflicts and distortions in the paper's normal operation. Editors must concern themselves with payoffs to reporters, not because it's bad journalism but because it's bad business. There are subtler implications as well: according to one editor, reporters are sometimes promoted or given special beats according to their ability to bring in political advertisements. Eager, young reporters learn to hustle after gacetillas, since they bolster the paper's revenue and make the reporter — and the reporter's immediate editor — look good. A reporter who dedicates special effort to establishing good contacts often ends up using them to coax ads from press chiefs. Given the number of newspapers in Mexico City competing for gacetillas, a hustling, well-connected reporter in a lucrative beat can be a real boon to a newspaper.

The relationship, of course, works both ways. Press officers with lucrative beats have a great deal of input in approving or vetoing reporters sent to cover their *fuentes.* Thus, journalists with a reputation for aggressive reporting can be refused politely by a press chief, who has thousands of dollars of gacetilla buying power to back up his opinion. "It's usually done on a very personal level," says the Mexico City broadsheet editor, explaining that if the editor sends a reporter considered to be ideologically unsuitable, "he might get a call from the press chief who'll say, 'Why'd you send me that guy? Why not send Paco instead?'"

Within the company, promotion to a "good" beat can be used to reward a reporter, just as assignment to a non-paying one can be a form of punishment. As a general rule, reporters receive a 15-percent commission on the gacetillas that come in from their beats; a recent innovation, pushed by some of the newspaper unions, stipulates a payment of 10 percent to the reporter and 5 percent to a "common fund" for all other employees. The common fund idea, instituted in an effort to redistribute the wealth earned from gacetillas, also broadens the base of employees with a vested interest in seeing the reporter bring them in. A reporter who imperils relations with a "good" source by printing aggressive articles or who, for reasons of principle or lack of hustle, doesn't bring in as many "ads" from a source as expected may even meet with criticism for endangering an important source of income for the paper and its employees. The reporter's journalistic talents risk being overshadowed by his or her ad-selling skills, as the latter are rewarded — monetarily, as well as by colleagues' approval — and the former, if not necessarily frowned upon, can get in the way.

The predictable result is often a distortion of the reportorial staff. Eager, hardworking reporters who know how to avoid offending key clients end up with the best-paying beats: certain ministries and, for example, the Mexican Petroleum Company (Petróleos Mexicanos — PEMEX). In the process, these well-paying beats collect a press corps accustomed to the rewards of non-critical reporting. Non-paying or low-paying beats, meanwhile, are considered backwaters. Areas that are important for their news value but that shun gacetillas — foreign relations is the commonly cited example — can have trouble getting good coverage and attracting top reporters, who for strictly financial reasons would generally prefer a less-important but better-paying beat.

The difference between having a "good" beat and a "bad" beat can be appreciated readily in the different standards of living of the privileged and non-privileged reporters. "When a reporter gets a good [well-paying] fuente, you can see it immediately in his clothes, the rings he wears and the car he drives," says the broadsheet editor.

The practice of rating reporters by their ability to draw revenue to the paper reaches grotesque proportions at some newspapers, where lists of the reporters' gacetilla earnings are posted alongside the earnings of other reporters at the paper and next to a chart showing the same fuente's purchases in competing newspapers.

The extra pay that gacetillas bring to the newspaper's employees, both directly and indirectly, is one of the strongest arguments in their favor for newspaper editors and publishers. Like tips for waiters, gacetilla commissions are considered a normal and legitimate "bonus" paid to staff members. It is a bonus, naturally, that allows the paper to save on payroll costs, though the results can be unsettling to an editor eager to enforce standards on his reporters. One editor says, "At any given moment, I have to be aware [when dealing with reporters] that the company in many cases is providing less than half their income. What's more, because of *embutes* (direct payoffs to reporters), I can never be sure how much they are earning from outside sources."

With the onset of the economic crisis in 1982, gacetillas became more important than ever for the survival of many newspapers; competition for them increased accordingly. The ex-press chief of a state government says, "Before the crisis, if the governor gave a big speech, it would be put on the front page of all the [capital] newspapers. Now with the budget cutbacks, they can't do that. Instead, they'll choose one of the mass circulation dailies, one influential broadsheet, one of the leftist papers and one of the rightist ones."

The economic pressures of the crisis have served to strengthen the arguments of those within any given newspaper who argue in favor of gacetillas. Besides relieving payroll pressures, publishing "paid" articles brings considerable revenue directly into the company's coffers. This, in turn, is used to justify a newspaper's principal goal: serving the readership. "Some editors will say, 'We can have more pages and expand news coverage for the readers,'" says the broadsheet editor. "It's a form of hypocrisy."

Nonetheless, changes are taking place in the handling of gacetillas that suggest that their days may be numbered, though no one expects them to disappear any time soon. Some newspapers have begun using slight, almost subliminal typographic changes to set gacetillas off from authentic articles. Some assign a different "font" (type style) to the headline or text. Occasionally, gacetillas are boxed off, though not consistently in any paper. One daily, the only paper with national distribution that consistently distinguishes gacetillas, sets the headlines of all gacetillas in italics.

It can be dangerous, though, to make gacetillas too distinguishable. A few years ago, one paper tried to identify paid insertions by putting "I.P." (*inserción pagada*) at the end of each one. The innovation was soon abandoned, presumably after clients balked at paying two to three times the going advertising rate for something that essentially was marked as advertising.

Besides distinguishing gacetillas from genuine articles, some newspapers have begun restricting the types of paid announcements that they will publish. Although all newspapers have a basic policy against printing personal, false, uncredited or malicious attacks, many — for the right price and the right political motives — will make exceptions to their policy. Gacetillas that pose as the newspaper's own investigative reports have long served as a vehicle for low political blows and even career-ending denunciations. They function, in short, as the stage on which much of the cutthroat political competition of the nation is acted out.

Gradually, though, a handful, though by no means all, of the country's influential newspapers have begun to set informal guidelines for paid insertions. The most commonly cited requirement is that it be "innocuous" for the readers. The general manager of one of the newspapers that is trying to enforce this code draws a distinction between "black gacetillas" and "white gacetillas": "A black gacetilla would be a false denunciation of, say, fraud, in a public official; those, we are rejecting. A white gacetilla would be, for example, some minor official in the State of Mexico who gets named to some new post and wants his picture in the paper with a little article about his promotion. This guy is a nobody who otherwise would never get into our paper but is willing to pay to be put in. So why not?"

Many in the newspaper industry, including some of those who are working to eliminate defamatory gacetillas from their papers, nonetheless decry moralizing about the practice in general. "The same thing goes on in every country in the world — and I mean white *and* black gacetillas," says the general manager. Indeed, in the United States, newspapers compete for hundreds of thousands of dollars of government advertising known as "legals," though in theory there is no explicit exchange for favorable news coverage. In practice, though, papers that publish sympathetic editorials are sometimes rewarded with a larger share of legals. Finally, some Mexican editors argue that commercial advertising can also imply a compromise of journalistic principles and that, given the traditional importance of the state in the economy, refusing advertising from the government would be unrealistic. Indeed, with the passing of many state-owned companies and banks into private hands in the last few years, the government's role in purchasing gacetillas has been reduced.

Still, some editors look ahead to the day when gacetillas will be eliminated altogether. "It is, ultimately, our duty to tell the reader what is paid and what is not paid," says the broadsheet editor. "It is part of the process of professionalizing journalism in the country, and it is the responsibility of the reporters themselves." He suggests the formation of an association of journalists, structured after the bar for the legal profession. "They need to establish some minimum of quality control, and they have to practice some self-criticism," he says. "So far, they've been resisting; something in the back of their heads tells them that this process is going to mean a cut in income for them."

Newspaper companies, the broadsheet editor feels, also have to make a commitment to the professionalization of their staffs, providing better pay and rewarding good reporting. The government, too, should be searching for ways to eliminate gacetillas and "put an end to this source of corruption." Nonetheless, he puts little faith in either the truthfulness or the appropriateness of periodic official pronouncements declaring an end to payoffs and lucrative beats. "This change has to begin inside the world of journalism. Any change brought in or imposed from outside would not be authentic," says the editor.

As if heeding this advice, the Salinas administration has done little to initiate a new relationship with the press, opting instead to follow the media's lead on the issue of increased press professionalization. To this end, Salinas has quietly supported the changes that the journalists themselves think are important, such as a minimum wage for reporters. As for gacetillas, neither the government nor the journalists have been able to muster the enthusiasm or the courage for a change in this business-as-usual practice.

Even so, a change may already have begun inside the world of journalism that eventually will lead to the extinction of gacetillas. Bravery and financial independence — perhaps the two key prerequisites for denouncing gacetillas — already exist in the Mexican press. But a lasting solution to the practice will depend on a change in the newspaper-buying public. When an informed public chooses overwhelmingly not to buy gacetilla-ridden periodicals, the gacetilla will be dead. And informing the public means talking out loud and in print about one's colleagues and competitors. In the end, it seems, the lion must learn to eat its own flesh.

Section II

Broadcast News

Chapter 4

Sound Bites and Soap Operas:
How Mexican Television Reported the 1994 Presidential Elections

Barbara Belejack

For as long as he can remember, when Miguel Acosta turned on the television, there was Jacobo Zabludovsky, telling him what the president had done that day or what new project the secretary of agriculture had inaugurated in some remote corner of Mexico. Throughout the 1994 presidential campaign, Acosta saw even more of the taciturn anchor of Televisa's "24 Horas" newscast along with Zabludovsky's counterpart on "Hechos," the fledgling competition on the recently privatized Televisión Azteca. As director of the media monitoring project for the Mexican Academy of Human Rights (the Academy), Acosta taped, analyzed and reported on the electoral coverage of Mexico's television newscasts. He did what no one in Mexico had done before — he painstakingly gathered evidence to prove what most people in Mexico had long suspected, that television coverage was highly skewed in favor of the ruling Institutional Revolutionary Party (Partido Revolucionario Institucional — PRI).

Acosta taped everything, from the last fading minutes of the *telenovelas* (soap operas) that led into the news, to the endless commercials for Pedro Domecq brandy. He taped entire newscasts, incidentally chronicling Televisa's self-promotion along with its biased election coverage. The newscasts

Barbara Belejack has reported on Mexico since 1988 for Newsweek, Mexico Journal *and other publications. She now works as a free-lance writer in Mexico City and teaches a course on the United States, Latin America and the media at New York University in New York.*

included such newsworthy items as Jacobo Zabludovsky's visit to the home of a 95-year-old vendor of a Televisa-owned tabloid; a Televisa soap star's visit to war-torn Armenia (despite electricity shortages, the soap must go on); an art exhibit at the Televisa-owned art museum; a Televisa soap opera based on the life and times of prerevolutionary dictator Porfirio Díaz (a major news story three nights in a row); a *New York Times* article about the Televisa telenovela; a retrospective on the 25th anniversary of the Apollo moon landing, featuring film clips of Zabludovsky and his then-sidekick, former Televisa executive and now Senator Miguel Alemán with John Glenn and Soviet cosmonauts; and a roundtable with six commentators discussing the merits of the new Mexican-Argentine tango association (Zabludovsky is a big tango fan). The ultimate "24 Horas" news story may have been an appearance by Lupita Jones, the first Miss Mexico to win the Miss Universe pageant. When Lupita visited the set of "24 Horas" to promote a new (Televisa-sponsored) beauty pageant, anchor Zabludovsky interviewed her on the air.

As fascinating as all this might be to students of contemporary Mexico, Acosta and his colleagues analyzed only election coverage, in the language of technocrats — numbers, pure and simple. They timed and classified stories according to a methodology Acosta had developed. Did the candidate appear in the opening summary of the broadcast? (Ernesto Zedillo, the PRI candidate, almost always appeared in the opening summary. Moreover, news of his campaign activities almost always appeared first in the segment on electoral news.) Did viewers hear the candidate's voice when they saw his image on the screen, or did they listen to a reporter or anchor's voiceover? Were the stories positive or negative? How much television time did each candidate receive? This was far more complicated than it might seem. There were nine presidential candidates in the 1994 election, including a contingent dubbed the *chiquillada*, representatives of parties with little popular support but significant government funding. These candidates served as spoilers; their sound bites were frequently used to convey negative messages about the major opposition candidates, Cuauhtémoc Cárdenas of the Democratic Revolutionary Party (Partido de la Revolución Democrática — PRD) and Diego Fernández de Cevallos of the National Action Party (Partido Acción Nacional — PAN).

In the spring of 1994, the Academy issued its first report documenting the extent to which political reporting on Mexican television was biased in favor of the PRI. The report concluded that the PRI received 43 percent of the total time devoted to presidential campaign news; when a candidate appeared in the first five minutes of the newscast, 91 percent of the time it was the candidate of the PRI. The PRI candidate appeared with simultaneous voice and image far more often than the opposition candidates.

In 1988, television coverage of opposition candidates was virtually nonexistent. According to a university study published after the elections, more than 80 percent of the air time devoted to electoral coverage went to the PRI. Throughout that campaign season, the late Manuel Clouthier, presidential candidate of the PAN, criticized Televisa for its pro-PRI bias. Clouthier led PAN supporters in demonstrations at Televisa's Mexico City headquarters and advocated an advertising boycott of the media giant. But as protests against the results of the 1988 election waned, so did protests against Televisa. In the wake of controversial mid-term elections in 1991, the Academy had begun monitoring media coverage and published studies showing pro-government bias in state elections in Michoacán, San Luis Potosí, Tamaulipas, the state of Mexico and Yucatán.

Nevertheless, it was not until 1994 that the media became a major issue in the Mexican elections, largely as a result of the work of Miguel Acosta and the Academy of Human Rights, one of a multitude of non-governmental organizations affiliated with the election watchdog, Civic Alliance (Alianza Cívica). Television — in particular, Televisa — was both medium and message during the 1994 elections, a protagonist in what Civic Alliance Director Sergio Aguayo Quezada called "the telenovela about Mexico's transition to democracy."

With the onset of the Chiapas rebellion, the presidential campaign was no longer the lead story on the nightly news. The assassination of PRI candidate Luis Donaldo Colosio on March 23, 1994, however, changed the equation. In his first month as a candidate, Ernesto Zedillo received three times as much coverage as Colosio had received in three months and twice as much coverage as Fernández de Cevallos and Cárdenas had received during the Academy's four-month study. For an entire week after Zedillo was selected as the new PRI candidate, Televisa broadcast clips of Colosio speeches before every commercial break. The clips were preceded by computer graphics of an enthusiastic Colosio smiling and waving his arms. The computer graphics were often preceded by news stories about the new candidate, portraying him as "the poor boy who made good," the personification of the Mexican dream and heir apparent to the murdered/martyred Colosio.

On May 12, 1994, Mexico officially entered the age of sound bites and electronic campaigns. After months of negotiations, the presidential debate that Colosio had initially proposed finally took place. Although technically it was not a debate, it would change political campaigns in Mexico forever. Almost immediately, political pundits determined that Fernández de Cevallos had "won"; before the debate, the PAN candidate had far less name recognition than his two principal opponents. After the debate, his standing rose dramatically in the polls. With his beard, gravelly voice and omnipresent cigar, Fernández de Cevallos had the "right stuff" for television. As a veteran litigator and legislator, he was adept at the one-two verbal punch. In contrast to Zedillo and Cárdenas, he used his television time to attack his opponents directly. He chided Cárdenas for his PRI past and leveled Zedillo with the charge that he was "a good boy who got good grades," a good boy whose "plan has left 40 million in poverty." For the rest of the campaign, Fernández de Cevallos pressured Zedillo for another debate, but the PRI insisted there wasn't enough time.

Although the second debate never took place, all nine presidential candidates appeared on the same stage in early June for a luncheon with Mexico's media elite, including Jacobo Zabludovsky. The occasion was the annual "Día de la Prensa" celebration. The press day ceremony was another opportunity for the presidential candidates to pitch their cases. Cárdenas spoke first and immediately tried to compensate for his lackluster debate performance: Mexico wouldn't have the kind of accurate, far-reaching information it needed, he said, "as long as the vast majority of televised messages that today saturate our homes obey the political objectives of the ruling party. Televisa — let's be clear about it — is one of the pillars of the authoritarian regime from which we all suffer."

"Every '24 horas,'" Cárdenas continued (pun intended), "democratic options are discredited … the true nature of our social reality is covered up, and there is an attempt to confuse the public about the nature of the political struggle for clean and fair elections."

That night on "24 Horas," Zabludovsky broadcast excerpts of the candidates' press day speeches, including the Cárdenas speech. He omitted the PRD candidate's reference to "every '24 horas'" and wrapped up the story with an editorial aside, commenting that Zedillo was the only candidate to offer concrete proposals and to be interrupted by applause.

The following day, Cárdenas held one of the largest rallies of his campaign, a "comeback" bid at Mexico City's National Autonomous University, a stronghold of PRD support. The main story on "24 Horas," however, was Zabludovsky's 22-minute live interview with Zedillo (another media first), an opportunity to ask the candidate how his campaign was going and what his family life would be like if he became president: "All your married life you have been an exemplary, close family. We noted that during your time as education minister and in other important positions, you generally ate at home. …" As Fernández de Cevallos later complained, there was a tendency among broadcast interviewers not only to treat Zedillo as the president, but "to elevate him to a god."

Even the gods, however, must take a back seat to soccer during the World Cup games. For several weeks during the summer of 1994, Mexico was held hostage to the World Cup games in the United States. The fate of former Argentine soccer star Diego Armando Maradona received far more attention than the fate of Diego Fernández de Cevallos or the unexplained sudden resignation (and subsequent return 48 hours later) of Mexico's Minister of Internal Affairs Manuel Camacho.

Competition between Televisa and Televisión Azteca in the political arena was tepid at best (the two newscasts didn't really compete with each other, since they were broadcast an hour apart), but when it came to soccer coverage, the competition was intense. Televisa and Televisión Azteca sports reporters battled it out for locker room access to the Mexican team. The Mexico City daily *Reforma* polled readers on their preferences in televised soccer coverage. (Televisión Azteca ended with a highly respectable 44 percent, a substantial improvement over its audience for the presidential debate.)

Foreign journalists began suggesting that the PAN candidate was losing the edge he had gained after the May debate. PAN strategists insisted that Fernández de Cevallos was simply responding to the natural order of things — no one could possibly focus on the Mexican presidential campaign until the World Cup was over. Typical campaign coverage (for all candidates) consisted of watching the candidate watch the Mexican team.

When Mexico beat the heavily favored Irish team early in the matches, Televisa arranged for a telephone hook-up so that Zedillo (who was fond of saying that the TRI, as the Mexican team is known, and the PRI were the best teams) could be heard on the evening news offering his congratulations.

When Mexico tied Italy, President Salinas did the calling. When Bulgaria ended the Mexican team's chances of advancing to the finals, a philosophical Ernesto Zedillo was quoted in the Mexican press as saying that soccer was a sport and had nothing to do with politics. However, the capital's most acerbic columnists lost no time in identifying the malady that plagued the Mexican team — Mejía Barón Syndrome, the unwillingness of the Mexican coach to send in fresh players, especially the highly touted Hugo Sánchez, in the final moments of play. Their message to the electorate was clear: beware of Mejía Barón Syndrome — don't be afraid of change.

While soccer entranced the Mexican electorate, Acosta and his team continued working in their cramped office on Calle Filosofía y Letras in the southern quarter of Mexico City. Armed with two VCRs and a fast-forwarding machine, they expanded the project to include monitoring of Multivisión (available by satellite to subscription clients), Channel 11 (a university-operated channel) and the morning and early evening newscasts of the two commercial networks. Mexico's Federal Election Institute (Instituto Federal de Elecciones — IFE), disturbed by the reports coming out of the Academy, warned the media to balance election coverage. The IFE also began its own monitoring project. Not surprisingly, the IFE report substantiated the Academy's conclusions: media coverage was biased in favor of the PRI.

Civic Alliance's Director Aguayo described the problem with television in soap opera terms. "After much hard work and endless adventures," he wrote, "society has managed to show who the bad guys are — the ones who never stop laughing, the ones who are always so sure of their power. It's the final episode, and society is watching the governor, who must choose between two private businesses and society. As always, we'll find out what happens right after these messages."

Lawyers for the Civic Alliance concluded that there was no legal remedy to force Televisa and Televisión Azteca to provide fair and objective coverage of the presidential campaign. Aguayo insisted, however, that if nothing were done, it would prove to the Mexican public that once again the rich and powerful were above the law. "For many," he wrote, "it would be proof that the only alternative lies in armed insurrection."

During this particular episode of the telenovela, Aguayo and others from the Civic Alliance met with President Salinas and presented him with a video of newscast excerpts. Not long after, Televisa magnate Emilio Azcárraga was seen entering Mexico's Ministry of Internal Affairs. Televisa issued a bulletin announcing its decision to grant free 15-minute blocks of time to all presidential candidates, while insisting that the network had always covered the campaign "with great care." Televisión Azteca extended a similar offer to all political parties.

By mid-July, the Academy noted that both "24 Horas" and "Hechos" were more objective in their presentation of campaign news. At the same time, analysts warned, since that improvement was based on nothing more than good faith on the part of the networks, the trend could easily be reversed. Around this time, the Academy also began examining paid political advertising and discovered a disturbing pattern.

The PRI had been broadcasting campaign spots with ordinary citizens who explained why they were voting for Zedillo. The spots did not indicate that they were paid for by the political party. What was the real relationship between the network and the party? Moreover, what was behind the blitz of strong pro-government advertising? The Academy calculated that in a single week, the PRI spent 5 percent of the maximum-allowed campaign budget on television advertising alone, a statistic that prompted the authors of the study to wonder whether the PRI was really paying for the spots in accordance with campaign regulations.

In addition, Zedillo benefited from television advertising campaigns promoting Mexico's anti-poverty programs, which critics had long insisted were disguised political advertising. By law, the advertising of programs such as Procampo and Pronosol Forestal (agricultural and community reforestation programs) was prohibited as of August 1, providing tacit acknowledgment at least of their political/electoral nature. Immediately after the advertising ban went into effect, the president and several cabinet members began storming the country in a last-minute spending blitz in some of the more impoverished rural areas, guaranteeing favorable prime-time television coverage for the ruling party.

As election day approached, attention was focused on the historic heart of the country, the Zócalo, or main plaza of Mexico City, and the final capital appearances by the three major candidates.

The *cierre*, or closing of the campaign, was a mix of old-style and new-style Mexican politics: old-style, because it was a remnant of the not-so-distant past when the objective of the presidential campaign was to provide an opportunity for the PRI candidate to get to know the country he would soon be governing by putting him through an exhaustive series of face-to-face meetings, from marginalized urban areas to the most remote rural villages; old-style, because the *cierre* was based on the most fundamental element of old-style Mexican politics — how many people can you get, one way or another, to stand in a plaza and cheer a presidential candidate? The *cierre* reflected new-style politics because Televisa and Multivisión made history by providing live coverage of the Zócalo campaign speeches of Cárdenas, Fernández de Cevallos and Zedillo.

The two opposition candidates ended their Mexico City campaigns on August 13, 1994, the 473rd anniversary of the fall of the Aztec capital of Tenochtitlán to Spanish troops under the direction of Hernán Cortés. As Cárdenas supporters began filling the Zócalo on the morning of the 13th, *concheros* (shell dancers, urban Mexicans who have tried to resurrect pre-Hispanic ceremonies) danced, drummed and burned copal incense just beyond the Zócalo. Cárdenas supporters perched on bleachers that were not really bleachers. "Prensa! Prensa!" called one to a television cameraman in the plaza, wanting to show the world, or at least that particular representative of the Mexican media, that he and the rest of the crowd were sitting on uncomfortable narrow iron tubes. Bleacher seats did not appear until the next day, just in time for the Zedillo rally. Another supporter voiced his objection to television coverage in general. "You think this is 7 percent?" he asked, referring to the candidate's standing in one pre-election poll. "Why do they just show Cárdenas' face? Why don't they ever show the crowds on television? Why is it that when they show Zedillo, they show crowds out to the mountaintops?" The candidate himself used the occasion to launch one more attack against Televisa, prompting a roar from the crowd.

Hours later, the yellow balloons of the Cárdenas campaign and the banners proclaiming "Change is peace!" were swept away. They were replaced by the white and blue logos and "Diego: The only safe change!" of the PAN. Blue and white paper ballots rained on the Zócalo as Diego supporters marched by chomping cigars and sporting fake Diego beards. The concheros were still dancing and drumming, but the concheros and PANistas were in two different worlds; the sounds of mariachi music ("Guadalajara!") and bullfight music blared from the PAN sound system.

The following morning, the Zócalo changed colors once again as the blue and white was replaced by the national colors — red, green and white, also the colors of the PRI. If the crowd did not extend to the mountaintops, it certainly did extend to the streets leading out of the Zócalo. Cameras (each party was allowed to film its own closing) focused on crowd shots, views of perfectly color-coordinated contingents of unions and other PRI organizations. Throughout his campaign, Zedillo had experimented with various slogans: "For your family's well-being!" "Ernesto Zedillo — He knows how to do it!" and "I'm voting for peace!" But the most prominent slogan in the Zócalo that day was the one that adorned the stage where a handful of luminaries, including soccer star Hugo Sánchez, were seated. The slogan was simple and to the point: "Vamos a ganar!" (We're going to win!)

On August 16, 1994, the Academy presented a final media monitoring report. Acosta and his team noted that "the improvement detected in electoral coverage ... has been reversed in this final stage of the political campaign, which is the most decisive moment in the electoral process. Television newscasts continue violating the right of Mexicans to information ... they continue to fail to present the various candidates in a balanced and objective manner."

Chapter 5

The Eye of the Tiger:
Emilio Azcárraga
and the Televisa Empire

Marjorie Miller and Juanita Darling

D ressed in their finest suits, 200 of Mexico's most successful and influential entrepreneurs gathered in Monterrey, Mexico, in 1990 to question President George Bush and top U.S. trade officials about American protectionism. They were the captains of Mexico's steel and cement industries, leaders of immense financial empires — real Mexican money assembled at the exclusive Casino Monterrey in a room with crystal chandeliers that nearly trembled amid so much power and privilege.

And yet, even in this group of titans, one businessman stood out with the blunt, self-assured way that he spoke to U.S. officials. Tall, broad-faced, with a dramatic shock of white through his dark hair, Mexico's leading media magnate rose to address then-U.S. Secretary of Commerce, Robert A. Mosbacher.

"I am Emilio Azcárraga Milmo, a communications entrepreneur, and my company is Televisa," he said in a booming voice. "For many years, we have enjoyed a special kind of free market in television transmission between the United States and Mexico, importing and exporting signals by satellite." However, he added, foreigners are not allowed to control stations in the United States.

Marjorie Miller was formerly the Los Angeles Times *bureau chief in Mexico City and now reports from Jerusalem. Juanita Darling was a* Los Angeles Times *business writer based in Mexico City and is now Central America bureau chief, based in San Salvador.*

"We were asked to leave the United States a couple of years ago. Now, we want to return. Will you be negotiating the structure of television license ownership in the United States?" he asked.

This was straight talk from a Mexican businessman. If you want a free trade agreement, he was telling U.S. officials, put your money where your mouth is. Open your borders. Let us buy American television stations.

In the big league of media barons, Azcárraga is right up there with Rupert Murdoch. With a near monopoly on broadcast television and a corner on the cable market, he is arguably as powerful in Mexico today as William Randolph Hearst was at the peak of his sensationalist American print empire. Azcárraga's $2-billion company — the world's largest producer and exporter of programming — makes and breaks Latin American television stars, controlling its actors just as the big Hollywood studios did in their heyday.

Azcárraga's power extends well beyond the entertainment industry. He is an unwavering ally of former President Carlos Salinas de Gortari and Mexico's system of one-party rule. Televisa is so close to the government that it is sometimes snidely referred to as the Ministry of Culture. With its vast reach and resources, the company virtually defines what is news in Mexico and, just as important, what is not.

"Imagine if ABC, CBS and NBC were one company," says Mexican media critic Raúl Trejo Delarbre. "That is what Televisa has been in Mexico. Lack of competition has permitted the great political and cultural influence of Televisa."

Unrestrained, the giant flourished under the country's old closed economy, but times are changing in Mexico. Salinas opened the door to outsiders. Ironically, the very free trade agreement that Azcárraga seeks to use to make his way back into U.S. Spanish-language television could also introduce real competition for him at home.

But some businesspeople and media observers believe he is unprepared for the challenge. Azcárraga's autocratic style is hardly compatible with competition and the openness required of a public company, they say. Would-be competitors point to disasters Azcárraga has wrought when trying to operate in the United States, where he does not enjoy cozy government relations and a home-court advantage.

During the 1960s and 1970s, Azcárraga built up a profitable 12-station Spanish-language network in the United States. But he was forced to sell in 1986 after the U.S. government accused him of illegally controlling the stations — a violation of foreign ownership laws. Azcárraga's interests in four stations were distributed among his U.S. partners; the $600 million that Hallmark Cards Inc. paid him for the remaining eight stations and the network, plus continuing fees for programming, helped finance his other U.S. ventures. In 1990, without so much as a market study, Azcárraga launched the *National*, the only nationwide sports daily in the United States. The paper folded in June 1991, after hemorrhaging $100 million.

When it comes to his private life, Azcárraga is more of a Howard Hughes than a Murdoch. Public appearances like the one in Monterrey are rare. He is a media mogul who shuns the press; consequently, little is known about him. Even his age is such a well-kept secret that when his nephew, Televisa vice president Emilio Diez Barroso, is asked about it, he blushes and stutters as if he has been queried on a particularly embarrassing subject.

Azcárraga mythology has filled the information void. Mexicans love to gossip about his yachts and paintings, his four marriages, his much-discussed vanity and obsession with youth. Friends describe Azcárraga as charismatic and generous, the benevolent patron of the hacienda. Others, who do not necessarily mean to be unflattering, describe him as autocratic and despotic. This is, after all, a culture that appreciates a strongman. Azcárraga's public nickname is "El Tigre" (the Tiger).

Many speak of him with a great deal of fear, which his family dismisses as perfectly natural. Another nephew and vice president, Alejandro Burillo, says, "When a man is important, people are afraid of him. Emilio is an important man in this country."

Few would argue that. His network is a unifying if not always an edifying force in a diverse country that has three times as many television sets as telephones. Farmers in remote mountain villages gather around the community television to watch the same soap operas, comedies and variety shows viewed in the living rooms of downtown Mexico City. When the government launched a birth-control program in the mid-1970s, Televisa debuted a soap opera, "Accompany Me," that encouraged its predominantly Catholic audience to engage in family planning. Contraceptive sales increased significantly during the months the program aired.

Mexican popular culture has long been shaped by the Azcárraga family. Azcárraga's father, also named Emilio, started the empire with a chain of radio stations. He introduced trumpets into the classic Mexican mariachi band in the 1930s so that the music would sound livelier on radio broadcasts. Today, a mariachi without horns isn't a mariachi.

Televisa owns two of the country's top soccer teams and made soccer the number-one sport on television. However, after a dispute with the Mexican Soccer Federation, the company stopped broadcasting all games except those of its own teams and began to promote bullfighting as Mexico's national pastime. Most of its sportscasts now begin with reports on bullfighting, usually at Mexico City's Plaza de Toros, operated by Televisa.

Azcárraga has brought high-brow culture to the middle and upper classes. Televisa stations promote exhibits — from Alexander Calder to Frida Kahlo — at the company-owned Cultural Center for Contemporary Art and provide a forum for intellectual discussions. Not everyone has equal access to Televisa microphones, however. Azcárraga's friend, Nobel laureate poet Octavio Paz, is routinely promoted, while renowned leftist writer Carlos Fuentes seldom is seen. And Azcárraga tries to define Mexican culture for the rest of the world as well. His "ECO" news programs are broadcast on Spanish-language television in the United States, Europe and Latin America, as are Televisa-made entertainment shows, especially soap operas. He also sponsored the lavish traveling art exhibit, *Mexico: Splendors of 30 Centuries*, which opened with Azcárraga and President Salinas in attendance at the Los Angeles County Museum of Art. The exhibit, which also traveled to New York's Metropolitan Museum of Art, was the most comprehensive collection of ancient, colonial and modern Mexican art ever assembled in the United States.

Azcárraga formed the Los Angeles-based foundation, Friends of the Arts of Mexico, to finance the multimillion-dollar show and was a major contributor. Not by accident, the show coincided with Salinas' efforts to raise Mexico's international profile and integrate the country into the world economy. Culture is one of Mexico's strongest selling points, and Azcárraga is one of Mexico's top salesmen. UC-Berkeley historian Alex Saragoza, who has studied Televisa, says, "They are trying to refute the negativism that characterizes the image of Mexico in the United States: drugs, corruption, electoral fraud. They sense the need to rehabilitate Mexico's image, and who better to do it than Televisa?"

Friends and family like to portray the billionaire as a regular guy who enjoys Chinese takeout on Sunset Boulevard as much as eating at the Bistro garden in Beverly Hills, who shops at Tower Records, goes to movies and nibbles popcorn. Of course, Azcárraga flies to and from his Hollywood home in a private Grumann jet, owns a 1,980-foot, custom-designed yacht and decorates the walls of his Mexico City mansion with works by Pablo Picasso and David Hockney. His dinner wines run $500 a bottle. But he also occasionally rides the Mexico City subway — unheard of among the upper crust — or visits the outdoor Lagunilla market to mix with the masses. Azcárraga drives himself about town in an armored grey Mercedes-Benz without the security entourage that usually accompanies other members of Mexico's business elite.

There may be richer men in Mexico, but family fortunes are closely guarded secrets; *Forbes* deduced Azcárraga's worth from documents required to prepare Televisa's stock-market registration.

Friends tell stories of Azcárraga reaching into his pocket to help out a sick employee or a waiter in financial straits. The 80-year-old shoeshine man who used to polish Azcárraga's father's boots still calls the media mogul "little Emilio," they say, and is the one person permitted to enter Azcárraga's office without knocking. The *only* one.

More common are the stories about Azcárraga's arrogance. A former producer recalls the time Azcárraga ordered all employees to wear a company badge at work, then fired a security guard who, recognizing the boss, allowed him into his own building without a security badge.

Others recount the tale of Azcárraga's oversized chair. The history of the giant wooden chair changes a bit with each telling, but the chair's purpose is clear — to humiliate. Azcárraga's father, the founder of Televisa, had the chair built so that a person sitting in it could not touch his feet to the floor. When Azcárraga inherited the leadership of the company, he also inherited the chair. Critic Trejo says, "Someone comes to him with a complaint, he seats them in the chair and says, 'It's too big for you, isn't it? When it isn't too big for you, we'll talk.'"

Some of those who know Azcárraga attribute his brusqueness to this relationship with his father. The senior Azcárraga, respectfully known as Don Emilio, was a streetwise, self-made millionaire who routinely referred to "my son, the idiot." Azcárraga has spent much of his life trying to prove his father wrong, friends say. Don Emilio, described by his grandchildren as a brash man with big hands that he used to clap acquaintances on the back, got his start as a salesman — first cigarettes, then shoes, then RCA Victor Gramophones and radio ads. He married a woman from San Antonio, Texas, and, according to a family friend, the young Emilio was born in August 1930, on the day that Don Emilio started his first radio station, XEW.

During the 1940s, the senior Azcárraga built Churubusco Studios, launching the Golden Age of Mexican cinema with stars Pedro Infante, Jorge Negrete and Dolores del Río. He also acquired one of the country's first television channels. In 1954 the precursor of Televisa, Telesistema Mexicana, was formed when Azcárraga, along with newspaper publisher Rómulo O'Farrill and inventor Guillermo González Camarena, merged their three nationwide channels into one network. The family of late Mexican President Miguel Alemán later bought out González's interest; Azcárraga added a fourth channel and changed the company name to Televisa in 1973, shortly after his father died.

In an era when revolutionary generals ruled Mexico, Don Emilio wanted his only son to become a soldier and sent him to a U.S. secondary school, Culver Military Academy in Indiana. However, the young Azcárraga never joined the military or even went to a university; he came home to the family business. As a young man, he enjoyed fancy cars and a privileged life, but that did not spare him from tragedy. His first wife, said to be his true love, died at 20. Azcárraga had four children by two more wives but lost a daughter in an automobile accident rumored to be a suicide. His only son, Emilio Azcárraga Jean, works for Televisa as vice president of programming. Azcárraga's fourth and current wife, Paula Cusi, a fashionable Mexican of Spanish descent, is said to be responsible for his interest and education in the arts. In her 40s, she is much younger than Azcárraga and part of what some consider his obsession with youth. "He is a grandfather, but he hates to be called that. He thinks it ages him," says an acquaintance.

Still, he is an imposing man who exudes power. Azcárraga inherited his father's business acumen along with his share of three television channels and two radio stations. He turned the company into the multifaceted empire it is today. With its four popular national channels, Televisa dwarfs the nominal competition. [See Jorge G. Castañeda on the sale of Imevisión.] In addition, Televisa owns Cablevisión, the nation's top cable company; six of the country's top radio stations, two record companies and a billboard advertising monopoly. The company makes movies and publishes books. Together, the Televisa companies rake in a phenomenal $4 out of every $5 spent on advertising in Mexico.

In 1990, Azcárraga split with partners Rómulo O'Farrill, Jr., and Alemán, in part because of the *National's* $100-million loss. Sources close to the company say Azcárraga took on the newspaper project alone but, when faced with heavy losses, declared the *National* a Televisa venture. O'Farrill reportedly showed up with ready investors and told Azcárraga to buy him out or be bought. Azcárraga bought. O'Farrill took a French restaurant, three houses in the Caribbean resort of Cancún, four automobile dealerships, a plane, a yacht and a rumored $350 million for his third of the company.

Alemán passed his interest on to his son, but the reorganization increased the Azcárraga family's ownership from more than one-third to about 80 percent. Azcárraga and his sister, Laura, kept Televisa; the other sister, Carmela, took the Mexico City cable company Cablevisión, which she later sold back to Televisa. Looking ahead, Azcárraga has begun gearing up to enter 21st-century businesses, from high-definition television to satellite telephones. Company officials have announced plans to raise $400 million by selling stock on the Mexico, New York, Tokyo and London exchanges.

Herman Von Bertrab, managing director of the San Diego-based *Bertrab Mexican Report*, says, "Televisa is going to change from a family-controlled company to a public company, and there will be some cultural clash. The records will be public, the numbers will be public, and they'll have to be acceptable to a board of directors, which the Azcárraga family will still control, but there will probably be some foreigners on it. Right now, everything is decided by Azcárraga." And he makes decisions quickly.

In Mexico's overly polite business world, where most people say only what they believe others want to hear, Azcárraga says exactly what he thinks.

Augustín Barrios Gómez, who worked at Televisa for many years in reporting and administrative positions, says, "If you give him an idea, he tells you right away if he buys it or if he thinks it's stupid. He never says 'Call me Monday.' It's either 'let's do it' or 'go to hell.'"

The bottom line, says a high-level government official who knows Azcárraga well, is that "Emilio talks to officials like no one else does. And he knows how to recognize talent. He takes what is of use to him and throws out what is of no use to him. He rewards loyalty and efficiency and punishes disloyalty."

Azcárraga is very clear about his own loyalties. Mexico's 1991 mid-term elections for a new Congress were important to President Salinas, who hoped they would be clean enough to demonstrate a commitment to democratic reforms while, at the same time, strengthening the Institutional Revolutionary Party's (Partido Revolucionario Institucional — PRI) majority in the legislature.

Three weeks before the vote, a reporter cornered Azcárraga at the annual Guelaguetza cultural festival in Oaxaca, where he was a guest of the governor, to ask about Televisa's biased campaign coverage. Azcárraga pulled no punches. "Televisa considers itself part of the government system and, as such, supports the campaigns of PRI candidates," he said. "The President of the Republic, Carlos Salinas de Gortari, is our maximum leader, and we are happy about that." After the vote, Televisa reported the PRI's sweeping victory in the federal elections but did not cover demonstrations in the states of Guanajuato and San Luis Potosí, where the opposition charged that the ruling party stole the governors' elections.

This alliance with the government has come under increasing criticism in recent years. After the 1988 presidential election, in which Televisa became an unofficial spokesman for Salinas, crowds protesting election fraud chanted "Death to Televisa." The conservative National Action Party (Partido Acción Nacional — PAN) printed bumper stickers that read, "Don't Watch Televisa. They Don't Tell the Truth."

Televisa serves the system, and the system serves Televisa. According to media expert Trejo, the government automatically renews Televisa's licensing. Although Mexican law allows no more than eight minutes per hour of broadcast time for commercials, the Ministry of Communications and Transportation routinely grants Televisa permission for more, sometimes as much as 20 minutes in an hour, according to Trejo. While prime time in the United States is from 8 p.m. to 11 p.m., Televisa calls prime time 6 p.m. to midnight and charges advertisers the higher rates for all six hours.

A law passed in the 1960s imposed a 25-percent tax on television earnings but allows Televisa to pay half its taxes with air time. Consequently, government ads are a common fixture on Televisa channels, in addition to the pro-government news coverage.

"The government and Televisa have an unwritten agreement to work together. But it isn't a total identification. There are some frictions," Trejo says. Azcárraga sought a cellular-telephone concession in Mexico, he says, and when the government didn't give it to him, the "24 Hours" news show began attacking the Ministry of Communications and Transportation in retribution.

Such tensions rarely surface over politics, however, because Televisa's view of the world is the same as the PRI's. News is official news. There is little, if any, debate of public issues on the airwaves, says Florence Toussaint, who covers Televisa for the weekly magazine *Proceso*. "Televisa minimizes contrary political positions. The values are those which prevail — authoritarianism. I don't think Televisa is proposing democracy. There is no attempt at objectivity. If they cover a march by teachers, it is about the traffic chaos they caused, not about their demands."

Televisa's coverage of the North American Free Trade Agreement (NAFTA) is similarly one-sided. The views of Mexicans critical of NAFTA, who fear U.S. domination of Mexico's economy, never appear in Televisa programs.

The Televisa reporter who strays from the party line pays a heavy price. A few months after taking office, Salinas ordered the arrest of the reputedly corrupt boss of the oil workers' union, Joaquín Hernández Galicia, known as "La Quina." The timing was perfect for Televisa newscaster Guillermo Ochoa, who had previously interviewed La Quina. But instead of getting kudos for showing the earlier footage on La Quina, Ochoa was fired. Azcárraga and the government decided the interview was too sympathetic to the union leader.

Asked about the firing, Emilio Diez Barroso, Televisa vice president of news and sports, says, "Emilio Azcárraga wanted a certain political tone managed, and he [Ochoa] wasn't in harmony with that tone." The incident illustrates Azcárraga's hands-on operation of the news department. Diez Barroso says that Azcárraga often presides over the Monday morning news meeting as well as over a Tuesday meeting for other programming.

Most of the Mexican media is managed by the government through a refined system of pressure, payoffs and self-censorship. With some notable exceptions, low-paid reporters receive the "envelope," payments from the government ministries and agencies they cover.

Televisa's solemn, bespectacled top anchorman for over 30 years, Jacobo Zabludovsky, is considered by some to be the Walter Cronkite of Mexico. Others dismiss him as a hopeless pawn in an undemocratic political system. When two reporters arrived at his office for a scheduled interview, Zabludovsky, wearing a jacket decorated with a map of the world, said, "I don't give interviews. I thought you wanted a tour of Televisa. What I have to say, I say on television." He quickly ushered them out in favor of another appointment, promising to meet again the following day. Later, he called to cancel.

Televisa has managed to combine its political partisanship with traditional Mexican values of family, loyalty and hierarchy to create commercial success. Even would-be competitors such as Ernesto Vargas, whose family owns an upstart pay-TV network called Multivisión, give the corporation its due.

"Televisa is an excellent company, efficient. It has done television very well," Vargas says. But he added that the techniques that serve Azcárraga in Mexico have not produced the same results in the United States. "Televisa is not prepared to compete. Where it has entered into competition, it has not done well."

In contrast with U.S. television, which courts sponsors, Mexican advertisers are at the mercy of Televisa. Either they buy a year of advertising in advance, before programming is determined, or they pay triple the standard rate, taking a chance they will get no air time at all. Sponsors are not advised, much less consulted, if their commercials are moved from one show or time slot to another. "They [Televisa] are able to dictate terms," says one advertising agency executive. "They changed the entire agency-client relationship, creating an atmosphere of fear and distrust."

Entertainers have even less clout. Working for Televisa means working exclusively for Televisa. This is not stated in actors' contracts, nor are they paid for exclusivity. But an appearance on one of the two government television stations or a role in somebody else's soap opera incurs the Tiger's wrath. The punishment is the veto, or blacklisting.

María Rubio speaks for many actors who have been blacklisted by Televisa. The 32-year Televisa veteran is best known for her role in "Wolf Cradle," a hit soap opera.

Over coffee on the patio of her condominium, which enjoys a view of Televisa's southern Mexico City studios, the strawberry-blonde actress recalls the incident that ended her career. After finishing "Wolf Cradle," she accepted an offer for a 12-hour series on Puerto Rico's Super-7 high-power channel. "I knew I was gambling with my career," she says. "My attitude was one of rebellion. I wanted to accept this opportunity. If all actors would do it, Televisa would have no choice but to accept things as they should be."

Back in Mexico, Televisa's doors were closed to her. Even theater managers said they could not cast her in plays because Televisa would refuse their advertising. She was finished. "I look upon this as a divorce," Rubio says. "I was married to Televisa for 32 years, and we had lots of children together — the shows I made. Now the man does not love me anymore. It's over."

Roberto Rivera, Los Angeles-based manager of the 13-member Salsa band, Banda Blanca, did not accept the veto so philosophically. In 1991, the band cut short a tour in Chicago to appear on Televisa's popular Sunday variety show, "Siempre en Domingo." But when they stepped off the plane in Mexico City, Rivera learned that their TV appearance had been canceled. Earlier that year, Banda Blanca had appeared on an awards show in Miami sponsored by *Billboard* magazine and a U.S. Spanish-language network. The program aired on Imevisión [the former state-run Mexican government network], and an angry Azcárraga reportedly banned all the artists on the awards show from Televisa.

Rivera was incredulous: "International artists have a right to work. Why must we bow to Mr. Azcárraga? What's going to happen where there's a common market if they can't accept competition? What happens if [a] Ted Turner comes in here?"

Faced with bad publicity over the issue, Miguel Alemán Magnani, Televisa vice president of corporate image, publicly denied that the artists were banned, and the company invited Banda Blanca to appear on another show, "La Movida." Officials also deny that the company keeps any kind of blacklist, but former employees and competitors confirm its existence. "We have had to pay more to people who fear being banned by Televisa because they work with us," said Vargas, the pay-TV network owner. "The fear costs us money."

When the government announced plans to sell one of its two national networks, Televisa Vice President Alejandro Burillo said that his company was actually looking forward to the competition when the government network is sold. "We are always the focus of criticism. Now there will be a point of comparison."

Despite such talk, Televisa's greatest successes in the United States came when the company operated as a Spanish-language monopoly north of the border. In 1961, while other Mexican businesses were content to serve a carefully protected domestic market, Televisa was buying up U.S. television stations. Azcárraga's network covered most Spanish-speaking regions of the United States by 1986, relaying Mexican-made programming to his U.S. stations through a sophisticated system in Laguna Niguel, California.

The technical success and expansion did not stop squabbles with his U.S. partners, who felt Azcárraga was taking an undue share of the profits. Then the Federal Communications Commission (FCC) accused Azcárraga of using a time-honored ploy for circumventing inconvenient laws restricting ownership: *prestanombres* or, literally, borrowed names. Azcárraga, as a foreigner, was limited to a 20-percent interest in the U.S. stations. The government charged that Azcárraga controlled them through in-name-only partners such as René Anselmo, a New York businessman who borrowed money from Azcárraga to buy off a 25-percent stake in the company. Under pressures from the commission, Azcárraga agreed to sell.

Meanwhile, Azcárraga has expanded into video stores, real estate development and publishing in the United States, with less than spectacular results. The *National* could not win enough readers away from the sports sections of local papers and specialty publications to build a circulation base, and it quickly folded. Azcárraga's high-toned marina at Battery Park in New York has also flopped. To head up the flashy development, Azcárraga chose former U.S. Ambassador to Mexico John Gavin, one of his best political contacts in the United States. The former actor seemed the perfect choice to sell slips for as much as $1 million each. In addition, Gavin had previously worked in Televisa's satellite communications subsidiary. The only problem, according to one company wag, was that "Gavin could not sell ice cream in Saudi Arabia."

However, these failed ventures are at the sidelines of what Televisa most wants to do in the United States: Spanish-language broadcasting. Televisa executives believe that if ownership restrictions are removed with the free trade accord, they can take charge of that quickly growing market as surely as they dominate Mexican television. The two U.S. Spanish-language networks, Univisión and Telemundo, are both losing money. There simply are not enough viewers and advertising dollars for two networks, much less three. But Félix Cortez, executive vice president of Televisa's ECO subsidiary, believes that Televisa has an edge.

"The problem is programming, and we have the production," says Cortez. "We're growing, and we must wait it out. There is a fixed amount of advertising dollars being divided among three. Someday it will be divided among two and then one. That is the law of competition."

That is the kind of competition Azcárraga envisions when he challenges the United States to open its borders: one huge company will dominate Spanish-language broadcasting, setting the cultural and political tone, dictating terms to advertisers and entertainers.

Editor's Note: A slightly different version of this article appeared in the *Los Angeles Times Magazine* in 1991. Since the article first appeared, NAFTA has become a reality. Televisa is now listed on the New York Stock Exchange. Contrary to the doubts expressed by some of the critics interviewed by Miller and Darling, Televisa and Azcárraga have emerged relatively unscathed by the increasing globalization of the media, in part because of their continued lock on the Mexican market and in part because of a series of alliances and purchases that occurred after this article was first published. Azcárraga and Televisa have entered into an alliance with Rupert Murdoch, for example. In late 1992, Televisa became 50-percent owner of Panamsat, a Stamford, Connecticut-based company that currently operates the main satellite used to beam programming into Latin America and will eventually provide worldwide coverage. Another Televisa investment was the American Publishing Group, the largest publisher of Spanish-language magazines in the world.

In place of the nominal competition from government-operated channels described by Miller and Darling, Televisa now faces nominal competition through Televisión Azteca, the recently privatized former Imevisión. Perhaps most significant, Televisa and Azcárraga have re-entered the U.S. Spanish-language television market, making the predictions by Félix Cortez, the Televisa executive quoted by Miller and Darling at the end of their article, chillingly accurate. Finally, 1993 produced even more evidence of the unwritten agreement between Televisa and the Mexican government when an embarrassing story came to light involving the promises of several of the most powerful businessmen in Mexico, most prominently Emilio Azcárraga, to spend millions of their personal fortunes to finance the PRI's 1994 presidential campaign.

When this article was first published, *Forbes* listed two Mexicans on its list of world billionaires. Azcárraga, whose personal fortune was estimated to be approximately $1 billion, was one of them. The most recent listing of world billionaires includes 13 Mexicans; Azcárraga's wealth is now estimated to be at least $5.1 billion.

Despite the changes that have taken place since this article first appeared, it remains a remarkable personal portrait of the man behind Televisa.

Chapter 6

Televisa North:
SPANISH-LANGUAGE NEWS
IN THE UNITED STATES

América Rodríguez

The long arm of Televisa reaches everywhere in the Spanish-speaking world. For most of its 33-year history, U.S. Spanish-language television has been the U.S. subsidiary of Televisa, the Mexican entertainment conglomerate. Throughout the 1960s and 1970s, the only Spanish-language news available in the United States was the distorted, censored news produced by Televisa in Mexico City. In 1981, the Spanish International Network (SIN), as Televisa USA was then called, produced the first national U.S. Spanish-language television news program, the "Noticiero SIN."

Though produced in the United States (first in Washington and later in Miami), this nightly broadcast remained very much under the thumb of Televisa editorial policy. In addition, it was riddled with intra-ethnic political rivalries. In 1986, under orders from the Federal Communications Commission (FCC), which found SIN in violation of the 1927 Communications Act prohibiting foreign control of U.S. broadcast outlets, SIN was sold to Hallmark Cards Inc. of Kansas City, Missouri. Hopes were high that once free of Televisa control, U.S. Spanish-language television (now called Univisión) would develop the incisive, reliable newscast desired by the U.S. Latino audience.

The "Noticiero Univisión" was a vast improvement over the "Noticiero SIN." With a budget almost ten times larger than that allotted by Televisa, the

América Rodríguez, formerly a correspondent for National Public Radio (NPR), teaches in the Department of Radio-Television-Film in the School of Communication at the University of Texas at Austin.

newscast was "modernized"; intra-ethnic rivalries were largely subsumed under U.S.-style journalistic "objectivity." The size of the audience tripled to about one million, and the news division began producing more programming as advertising revenue increased. But the hiatus from Televisa control only lasted six years. In 1992, Televisa regained control of Univisión with an FCC-approved ownership structure. Below the economic, historical and political contexts of U.S. Spanish-language television journalism are traced, the news produced in the Hallmark years is examined, and the effects of renewed Televisa control upon U.S. Spanish-language television journalism are discussed.

Economics

When Emilio Azcárraga (father of Televisa's current owner) opened the first U.S. Spanish-language television stations in 1961, KMEX-Los Angeles and KWEX-San Antonio, he had already built a vertically integrated monopoly of radio and television networks in Mexico. Artists under exclusive contract to Azcárraga would perform in Azcárraga-owned theaters; those performances would be broadcast on Azcárraga-owned radio and television stations. When Azcárraga moved north of the border, he simply expanded his monopoly into the United States.

The programming broadcast in the United States had already recovered production costs and turned a monopolistic profit in Mexico. For Televisa, the U.S. market is a nearly pure profit operation. In other words, Univisión is a secondary market twice over: secondary for the U.S. advertisers who disdain the Latino audience and secondary for Televisa, its principal program supplier. Univisión is twice marginalized within the increasing globalization of television. Although Latinos made up 9 percent of the U.S. population in 1992, U.S. Spanish-language television revenue totalled only 1 percent of all U.S. television advertising dollars, according to *Hispanic Business*.

The character of Televisa programming is a function of its institutional structures. "Noticiero Univisión" is produced under the same commercial constraints as the mainstream networks. The incentive is to create programming — including news programming — that is inoffensive, entertaining and designed to appeal to a panethnic U.S. Latino audience of Cubans, Puerto Ricans, Salvadorans and Guatemalans, as well as to a majority audience of Mexicans and Mexican-Americans.

U.S. Latino panethnicity is the dubious notion that all Latin American people, or people of Latin American descent who live in the United States, are one unified community and that the Spanish language erases profound differences in race, class and U.S. immigration history. This notion is the commercial foundation of the "Hispanic market" that sustains Univisión.

History: "Noticiero SIN" 1981-1986

In 1981, SIN began producing its own U.S. national newscast, "Noticiero SIN," which was broadcast on U.S. Spanish-language television stations, replacing "24 Horas" on most stations. SIN president René Anselmo said in a press release, "American media's coverage of events in Latin America tends to concentrate on earthquakes and coups, while the media's coverage of domestic news about Hispanics focuses on police reports. Now Hispanics are able to receive a Hispanic view of what is going on in the world."

Despite the panethnic intentions of the network president, "Noticiero SIN" was, from its inception, dominated by Televisa's journalistic philosophy and characterized by contentious intra-ethnic ideological battles.

Shortly after beginning nightly broadcasts from makeshift studios in Washington, the fledgling national news organization aired a report from El Salvador about that country's civil war. The report drew sustained and angry criticism from many in the audience who complained that it had a leftist slant and favored the insurgent Farabundo Martí National Liberation Front (Frente Farabundo Martí para la Liberación Nacional — FMLN) guerrillas. Despite the vigorous objections of SIN journalists, network president Anselmo went on the air to apologize for the report, saying, "the coverage of El Salvador has been biased" and promising that in the future "news reporting will be professional and unbiased." The SIN news director, furious that the network president would interfere with his journalistic autonomy, resigned in protest. This incident is remembered by Univisión journalists as an early declaration of their determination that U.S. Spanish-language television news be free from political interference.

The following year, "Noticiero SIN" moved to Miami where, according to former SIN journalists, the newscast began to express the fiercely anti-communist views of exiled Cubans and Nicaraguans. Mexican-American María Elena Salinas, then an anchor at the SIN affiliate in Los Angeles, KMEX-TV, regularly substituted for vacationing SIN anchors. Clearly uncomfortable with the memory, she carefully chooses her words when describing the Miami-based "Noticiero SIN," saying, "It was like a local newscast. It was geared to an audience with very specific ideas."

Her colleague at SIN, Univisión co-anchor Jorge Ramos, further explained that since SIN was based in Miami, where most of the Nicaraguan [and Cuban] exile community had developed, most people saw the network as pro-contra.

The journalists are less reticent about the "Zabludovsky affair," which they consider a victory and an affirmation of the objectivity and profession-alism of U.S. Spanish-language television journalists. In 1986, one month after the FCC-ordered sale of the SIN stations, Televisa's Emilio Azcárraga reas-signed Jacobo Zabludovsky — an icon of Mexican television news and anchor of "24 Horas" — to a new U.S.-based news service, Orbital Communications Company (Empresas de Comunicaciones Orbitales — ECO) that would absorb the SIN staff and broadcast in both the United States and Latin America. Half the "Noticiero SIN" staff resigned in protest. Just months earlier, Zabludovsky had presided over Televisa's (and SIN's) silence about charges of Institutional Revolutionary Party (Partido Revolucionario Institucional — PRI) electoral fraud in the border state of Chihuahua and demonstrations in Mexico City by the homeless after the 1985 earthquakes. The SIN journalists' outrage was fueled by the fact that these stories had been covered extensively in U.S. news media, including the mainstream television networks. Azcárraga backed down. Jorge Ramos states simply, "Zabludovsky never showed up."[1]

Univisión journalists' history of being buffeted by Latin American political actors from the left and right have made them ardent proponents of the First Amendment to the United States Constitution. "It's almost a religion for me," Ramos says, dismissing a suggestion that the U.S. government helps set the U.S. journalistic agenda, albeit in a manner less direct than that used by the Mexican government in setting agendas for Televisa. From the perspective of Jorge Ramos and other Univisión journalists who have worked in Latin America, the most important element of U.S. journalism is what they believe is its detachment from the U.S. government: "That's what I really appreciate about American journalism," Ramos explains. "It's great to see that freedom everywhere. When I had an interview with President Bush, they didn't ask me for questions beforehand. They just wanted to know generally what I wanted to talk about. They didn't censor anything or bug my phone. They just wanted to know the subjects, the issues, that's it."

This is not naiveté; elsewhere Ramos has spoken harshly of U.S. journalistic ethnocentrism. Rather, it is embracing an ideology that, from these journalists' perspectives, allows them to communicate professionally what they see as political reality. This is the "journalistic opportunity" that Ramos sought when he emigrated from Mexico to the United States.

Univisión journalists use the U.S. objectivity code to protect themselves from political pressures and to legitimize themselves as professional journalists. Adherence to what they understand to be key elements of U.S. journalistic objectivity — independence from state power, political detachment and neutrality — is what allows them to call themselves U.S. professionals. It is their proof of American-ness. This cloak of objectivity is the foundation of U.S. journalists' autonomous power. For Univisión journalists, their objective detachment is continuously challenged by their ethnicity and their minority status in U.S. society — and that of their imagined audience.

History: "Noticiero Univisión" 1987-1992

A fter the sale of SIN to Hallmark, the newly renamed Univisión network sought to redefine its audience in order to make it more appealing to advertisers. The network's own research indicates that the vast majority — perhaps as much as 70 percent — of Univisión's audience is made up of recently arrived and/or lower-middle-class immigrants. These television viewers are, because of their low incomes, a commercially unattractive group. Hispanic "ethnics," in contrast, have higher incomes, more disposable income and are consequently a more attractive audience to sell to in the marketplace.

Joaquín Blaya, the former chief executive officer of Univisión who now holds the same post with Telemundo, calls these viewers "born-again Hispanics." These are bilingual people who have been using more English-language than Spanish-language media but for a variety of reasons (affirmative action, racism, family concerns) have recently renewed their feelings of ethnic solidarity and, in the process, discovered Univisión.

The same market research that prompted Univisión executives to target "born-again Hispanics" stressed that middle-class U.S. Latinos like to watch the news. "Noticias y Más" ("News and More") was Univisión's version of "tabloid TV," focusing on "human interest" stories from the United States and Latin America. The news department began producing two editions of the nightly "Noticiero Univisión," one airing at 6:30 in the evening and the other at 10:30 p.m. "Portada" ("Cover Story"), an hour-long weekly program modeled on "60 Minutes," was Univisión's vehicle for longer investigative and feature stories. "Temas y Debates," a public affairs discussion program that originated with SIN, continues to be broadcast on Sunday morning. In addition, under Hallmark, Univisión allocated considerable resources — capital costs for the construction of new studios as well as for staff training — to the news departments of its nine owned-and-operated stations for local news and public affairs programming, which generally aired for from two to three hours daily.

This was a significant investment in news programming (five times the amount Televisa allocated to U.S. news production and an indication of Hallmark's determination to recreate U.S. Spanish-language television) and its audience.

To lure this "born-again Hispanic" audience, Blaya significantly changed the programming mix. When Hallmark bought Univisión, 90 percent of its broadcast day was filled with Televisa imports. By 1986, that figure had been reduced to 50 percent; the remainder of the programming, including the significantly increased news programming, was produced in the United States.

Univisión Journalists

"Noticiero Univisión" is produced by ethnics for immigrants. Many Univisión journalists are themselves immigrants — they were born abroad and are now naturalized U.S. citizens or permanent residents. However, I affix the label "ethnic" to emphasize these journalists' accommodation to and acceptance of mainstream U.S. political culture. They are navigating the cultural space between two cultures through the process of creating a third. "Ethnic," in this context, also has a class dimension: Univisión journalists, like other U.S. national broadcast journalists, are members of an elite class, both relative to the U.S. Latino population and to the general U.S. population. With few exceptions, Univisión journalists were professionally educated in U.S. university journalism schools and are currently receiving annual salaries that range from $40,000 to $110,000. Education and income have made them a part of the privileged sector of society. Race, language, national origin — that murky yet crystalline mixture of societal attributes defined as "minority" — are what marginalizes them.

Intra-ethnic rivalries are masked in Univisión entertainment programming or advertising. The illusion of U.S. Latino panethnicity is achieved by eliminating specific national origin cultural cues. (Denationalized "Walter Cronkite" Spanish and generic "Hispanic" symbols replace cigars and palm trees for Cubans or cactus and *ranchera* music for Mexicans.)

In contrast, news is mostly about politics. Differing political ideologies are at the root of most Latino intra-ethnic tensions and are not as easily disguised. As a result, Univisión journalists are simultaneously pulled toward two poles. The panethnic pole motivates production for a broad, unified community of interests, the imagined community that news director Martínez believes is more interested in Latin American news than European news. The other, counter-panethnic, pole pulls the journalists toward production for a more diversified, imagined community of interest: Mexicans and border issues; Puerto Ricans and the island's referenda; Cubans and the reshuffling of the Castro government. The examples that follow illustrate U.S. Latino intra-ethnic rivalries playing themselves out on the "Noticiero Univisión" terrain.

Challenges to "Noticiero's" U.S. Latino Panethnicity

Overall, about one-third of "Noticiero's" senior editors, producers and U.S.-based correspondents are Cuban-American. About one-half are Mexican-American, and about 15 percent are Puerto Rican. Clearly, relative to the U.S. Latino population and especially to the Univisión audience — which network executives estimate is about two-thirds Mexican and Mexican-American and about one-tenth Cuban-American and Puerto Rican, respectively — Cubans are overrepresented. Two of the three top Univisión news management positions are held by Cuban-Americans and none by Mexican-Americans.[2] Since the 1986 sale of Univisión to Hallmark, the network's news department has been the site of three public intra-ethnic clashes about news department staffing and program content.

The first came within six months of the naming of Cuban-American Guillermo Martínez as the network's news director. During the same period (late spring 1987), another Cuban-American was named general manager of the Univisión owned-and-operated station in Los Angeles, KMEX. About one-half the largely Mexican-American KMEX staff signed a petition protesting what they called the "Cubanization" of Univisión. Univisión denied any racial discrimination and pointed to "Noticiero" co-anchors Jorge Ramos and María Elena Salinas, who are Mexican and Mexican-American, respectively, as proof of the network's commitment to its largely Mexican and Mexican-American audience. At this writing, seven years later, the station manager of KMEX is also Mexican-American.

On November 5, 1991, a Cuban-born syndicated columnist, Carlos Alberto Montaner, as part of his regularly scheduled commentary segment on "Portada," Univisión's weekly newsmagazine, discussed why Puerto Ricans in the United States live in worse economic conditions than other Latino groups in the United States: "There is probably more than one explanation, but the one that seems most important to me is this: there is a grave family problem in the Puerto Rican ghettos of the United States, where there are thousands of very young, single mothers who try to escape poverty through welfare or through new partners who then leave, leaving behind other children to worsen the problem."

These comments provoked immediate outrage from Puerto Rican politicians and community leaders as well as from other, non-Puerto Rican Latino leaders. The critics said Montaner's comments were ignorant and insensitive at best. Most critics accused him of gross sexism and racism; many demanded his resignation. A coalition of New York City Puerto Rican organizations began an advertising boycott campaign directed at Univisión's New York station, WXTV. Although Montaner apologized for his comments on the following week's program, saying he had been misunderstood, Goya Foods, a Puerto Rican company that caters primarily to the Hispanic market, pulled its advertising from WXTV.

In reaction, news director Martínez complained that Montaner's comments were taken out of context. Pointing out that the controversial material was immediately rebutted by another on-air commentator, Martínez asserted that Montaner's piece was just "good, provocative journalism." He added, however, that some of Montaner's phrasing was too broad and thus open to criticism. Several Univisión journalists noted with wry grins that the Montaner-Goya incident significantly increased WXTV's ratings. The most recent public intra-ethnic/class antagonism incident involving Univisión news received less publicity than the two outlined above but was equally virulent. In January 1991, Univisión's national newsroom moved from Laguna Niguel, a Los Angeles suburb, to Miami. The reason for the move turned on logistical and economic factors involving aerial transportation routes (for taped reports from Latin America), time zones (most U.S. news occurs on Eastern Time) and real estate costs (Univisión already owned a suitable building in Miami). Martínez originally wanted to locate the national news headquarters in Washington because it is "neutral territory," meaning that unlike Los Angeles and Miami, there is no dominant Latino national origin group. That option was ruled out when it was determined that operating "Noticiero Univisión" out of Washington would have been significantly more expensive.

The move was controversial from its inception because, as one Mexican-American Univisión news staffer put it, "We are leaving behind most of the audience" — that is, the Mexicans and Mexican-Americans of the southwestern United States — and going to live among "the bad guys," the Cuban exiles of south Florida. "Noticiero" co-anchor Ramos recalled that in the 1980s a Miami-based "Noticiero SIN" was clearly biased in favor of anti-communism in general and the contras in particular. Consequently, he was leery of relocating "Noticiero Univisión" headquarters in Miami. "We were very concerned about being influenced by the Cuban community and their ideas," he said, "because those are their concerns and other communities have different concerns. We don't want a particular set of ideas to be dominant in the newscast."

"Noticiero" arrived in Miami in time for the start of the Persian Gulf War. Soon after the war began, Ramos became the target of an organized campaign by several Spanish-language radio stations in Miami — long established as among the more strident voices within the Cuban-American community. Announcers and callers to radio talk-show programs accused Ramos of being "unpatriotic." After several weeks, Ramos confronted his accusers by participating in one of the call-in programs. One caller insisted, "I am an architect and a Cuban, but I am first a Cuban and then an architect. And you are a journalist and a Mexican, and before being a journalist you are a Mexican — so I don't think you have any credibility."

To briefly decode what the caller was saying: "I am Cuban, anti-communist, and American and so, politically righteous. You, on the other hand, are Mexican, a commie-lover and have no business talking about my USA."

These three incidents bring into focus decades-old suspicions and resentments among Mexican-Americans, Puerto Ricans and Cuban-Americans. Moreover, considered in the context of U.S. Spanish-language media history, these incidents again illustrate that for Latino community leaders, media content is a central political issue. Further, they illustrate the potentially contentious nature of "Noticiero Univisión's" panethnic mission.

Most of the U.S.-based staff of "Noticiero Univisión" received their training in U.S. journalism schools. This schooling (later reinforced by journalism work experience) gives them a common professional culture that they share with other U.S. journalists. At its core is the ideal (or ideology) of professional objectivity: journalists should be neutral, nonpartisan, fair-minded chroniclers of the day's events.

Univisión journalists adopt the same objective narrative stance and embrace the same values, with one exception — ethnocentrism. This, of course, is not surprising, given that many of the journalists and most of the audience are immigrants and binational in outlook. Moreover, they are hyphenated Americans, members of "minority" communities and foreigners in their adopted land.

Univisión journalists experience this exclusion on a professional, as well as a personal, basis. For example, Univisión coverage of the Persian Gulf War was as uncritically flag-waving as that of any of the U.S. English-language networks. The form of Univisión's coverage mimicked that of the major U.S. networks, described by communications scholar Elihu Katz as "non-stop information without interpretation and non-stop interpretation without infor-mation." In addition, "Noticiero's" coverage of the Persian Gulf War featured its audience in their role as U.S. citizens in such stories as a profile of a Puerto Rican tank battalion in Saudi Arabia and another about an air force town in south Texas anxiously sending its young men and women off to war.

Yet even during this dramatic display of their "American-ness," Univisión journalists had to fight what they called "discrimination" in order to do their jobs. "Noticiero" co-anchor Jorge Ramos remembers, "Our correspondents in the Persian Gulf faced a lot of problems convincing the American military officers that Hispanics were part of the war. When our correspondent was part of the pool, he would report in English, but when other correspondents were asked to at least get an answer or two in Spanish [from the soldiers], they wouldn't do it. It was like Hispanics weren't part of the war, like Spanish was not one of the languages spoken. ...I think that was one of the things that didn't change from Vietnam to the Persian Gulf. Hispanics were used to fight on the front lines, but ... I suppose this happens with minorities in every country."

Univisión journalists cherish their Latino ethnicity; their work promotes and advances this identity. They also yearn to be accepted as Americans; their embrace of objectivity speaks to their desire to be accepted as professional *U.S.* journalists. Time and again, they are reminded that the dominant society does not recognize their existence nor that of their audience.

Univisión News

"Noticiero Univisión" — without the soundtrack — looks much like a mainstream newscast. There are two anchors (Jorge Ramos and María Elena Salinas) sitting behind a desk introducing taped reports. Univisión reports generally end with footage of a correspondent standing in front of an authoritative building such as the White House or the State Department. They cover much of the same territory as Univisión's mainstream counterparts, they are about the same length, and the discourse has roughly the same rhythm as mainstream reports. The duration of the sound bites and narration segments, as well as the camera angles and editing, are similar.

When one turns the volume up and hears the Spanish language, it is, of course, clear that this is not a mainstream newscast. However, if one were to listen closely to the Spanish, one would hear more profound similarities in the fundamental format of the journalism. The narrative stance of "Noticiero" correspondents is similar to that of the journalists of ABC's "World News Tonight," as are the story-telling conventions, and — at least in the reporting from Washington — the cast of characters is largely the same. Is "Noticiero Univisión" simply a Spanish-language translation of "World News Tonight"? The answer is, emphatically, no. The two programs' formats are nearly identical, and they share many aspects of a professional ideology. However, there are important points of departure.

The Univisión and ABC maps of the world — and, therefore, definitions of news — are vastly different. The broadest finding of comparative content analysis is that ABC produces a nationalist newscast; Univisión, an internationalist one.[3] Despite its name, three-fourths (77 percent) of the time on "World News Tonight" was taken up with stories about the United States. This includes stories about U.S. policy toward foreign countries. In clear contrast, 60.3 percent of "Noticiero Univisión" was devoted to news of countries other than the United States. Almost half (45.3 percent) of "Noticiero's" time was devoted to news about Latin America. ABC's nightly news devoted less than 1 percent of its airtime to Latin American stories during the same time period. Univisión's mapping of the United States was also quite different from ABC's: 14.5 percent of the Univisión nightly news, or about one-third of its total U.S. coverage, was about U.S. Latino communities. "World News Tonight" did not produce any stories about U.S. Latino communities, nor did any Latinos appear in the ABC nightly newscasts in May 1991 or June 1992.

Furthermore, the priority or value given to particular stories within the two networks' programs is markedly different. The first story of each newscast, what journalists call the "lead," is the story judged most important, most "newsworthy" for a given day.[4] Seventy-two percent (18 of 25) of ABC lead stories were "Beltway" stories, that is, stories that concern the president, the cabinet, the Congress or other federal agencies. Univisión journalists also give U.S. federal government news a high priority. Fifty-six percent (14 of 25) or slightly more than half of Univisión nightly news lead stories were also "Beltway" stories. Keeping in mind that some lead stories covered two or more topics, ABC's next-most-common leading story category was U.S. stories not as narrowly concerned with events within the Beltway, for example, unemployment or other aspects of the U.S. economy. In contrast, the second-largest category of lead stories on "Noticiero Univisión" was stories about Latin America.

With respect to format, the similarities between ABC and Univisión are as analytically important as are the differences in content. Every day "Noticiero Univisión" reproduces mainstream U.S. television news forms, adapting but not fundamentally altering them. As with Univisión journalists' interpretations of U.S. journalistic ideology, an examination of their reconstructions of standard U.S. television news forms illustrates the interaction of dominant and minority political cultures.

Univisión's production of U.S. Latino news highlights the defining tension that characterizes "Noticiero," the tension between the journalists' commitment to professional objectivity and their equally resilient professional commitment to their imagined audience.

U.S. Latino stories represent 16 percent of the "Noticiero Univisión" newscast — the largest single category of stories about the United States. These stories are consistently longer than all other "Noticiero" stories, a median of 143 seconds, compared to 26 seconds for general Univisión stories; the stories use roughly three times as many actualities as other "Noticiero" stories.

The social status of the U.S. Latinos who populate these stories is markedly different than that of the general U.S. "Noticiero Univisión" population. This reflects the generally lower social status of U.S. Latinos relative to the general U.S. population. U.S. Latinos tend not to be "news makers." Overall, 41 percent of Univisión U.S. news sound bites are of government officials, contrasting sharply with 28 percent of the U.S. Latino news sound bites. Further, 37 percent of U.S. Latino news subjects are "unknowns" or individuals with no public social position, compared to 28 percent of the overall sample of U.S. news subjects. Roughly three times as many sound bites were of Mexicans and Mexican-Americans than of either Cuban-Americans or Puerto Ricans — this approximates the demographics of U.S. Latinos and the findings of Univisión audience research.[5]

An examination of the content of "Noticiero's" U.S. Latino stories results in two broad category groupings. In the first, Latinos illustrate traditionally conceived U.S. news stories, such as those about the national economy, public school education or new discoveries in the health sciences. The second category of stories, principally concerning immigration from Latin America and U.S. Latino civil rights, is rarely included on the mainstream national news agenda.

Unlike U.S. government news, or U.S. election campaign news, there is no professional U.S. journalistic consensus about national U.S. Latino news. In fact, to the extent that this question has been addressed by mainstream national journalists, the consensus is that news about U.S. Latinos is *not* national news.[6] This is the case despite Census Bureau reports that Latinos compose 9 percent of the U.S. population and are projected to be the nation's largest minority group by 2030. There are, of course, exceptions. These occur when Latinos are actors in established news events, such as when high-ranking Latino officials "make news," for example, when Bush "drug czar" Bob Martínez announced the results of a study showing that illegal drug use among U.S. teenagers is declining. News about U.S. Latino *communities* is even less frequent. Increasingly, "Hispanics" are explicitly named as a "minority" group, as in "blacks and Hispanics."

U.S. Latino News

"Noticiero's" coverage of Latinos in the electoral arena of U.S. politics, as voters, candidates and elected officials, is Univisión's single-largest U.S. Latino news topic. It is a special case of the inclusive mode of U.S. Latino news discussed above. Similar in many ways to their coverage of the Persian Gulf War, Univisión journalists are supporters of U.S. electoral processes. In this, they are no different from their mainstream colleagues. It is "Noticiero's" unblushing advocacy of the inclusion of U.S. Latinos in U.S. electoral politics that sets it apart from its mainstream counterpart. To do otherwise, from the perspective of Univisión journalists, would be comparable to analyzing the desirability of social justice. The inclusion of Latinos as U.S. elected officials is a consensual public virtue (as was winning the Persian Gulf War) and therefore exempt from the norms of "objective" journalism.

"Noticiero's" U.S. Latino political coverage should be understood in the context of Univisión's U.S. political reporting in general: its focus is on the strategy and tactics of the campaigns and not on the social issues or social choices represented in the elections. This is the dominant mode of U.S. political journalism, particularly of U.S. television political journalism, often called "horse race" reporting.

Latin America News

Forty-five percent, or nearly half, of each "Noticiero Univisión" is about Latin America, while just over 1 percent of ABC's "World News Tonight" concerns news of Latin America, representing an enormous disparity in story selection and the most direct evidence of the distinct world views of these two U.S. television networks. Perhaps this is to be expected of a national news program that is produced for an audience made up largely of Latin American immigrants. However, it seems simplistically misleading to conclude that "of course" Univisión would give prominence to news of "home." Univisión's Latin American coverage positions its audience as residents of a hemisphere, what the journalists call *el continente americano*, the American continent. Univisión's drawing of the global map emphasizes the interaction of the nations of *el continente americano*. This global mapping defines U.S. Latino communities as a part of Latin American society. The journalists assume that U.S. Latinos are interested in Latin American politics as well as the Latin American Olympic medal count and the deaths of Latin American actors and artists. Mainstream U.S. newscasts draw their global maps with the United States at the center, Asia on one periphery and Europe on the other along an east-west global axis. The Univisión global axis runs north-south, through the United States to Mexico, Central America and South America.

By committing such a large proportion of its resources to Latin American news, "Noticiero" journalists, many of them immigrants themselves, are acknowledging the duality of immigrant, especially recent immigrant, life. Immigrants are *between* two countries, *of* two countries and not fully present in either. This is especially true of Latin American immigrants, many of whom, after "settling" in the United States, maintain close contact with their native countries, in many instances visiting frequently. Often this national duality is evidenced in the selection of the lead story for a given day's program. A single lead story is *not* selected; two are. For example, on March 17, 1992, "Noticiero" began,

> Jorge Ramos: Good evening. The primary elections today in Illinois and Michigan could decide which candidates will continue on to the finish line. Maria Elena Salinas: We will have extensive coverage of these elections later. But first, we go to Buenos Aires, Argentina, where this afternoon there were war-like scenes....

From the point of view of a Mexican immigrant, "Noticiero Univisión" offers little "news from home." Of the 25 or so stories on each newscast, perhaps one or two will be about Mexico. While Mexican news is the most represented of Latin American countries (22 percent of all Latin America stories), the news is largely about the politics of the federal government in Mexico City, which may or may not have a bearing on an immigrant's life or that of his/her family in Mexico. Still the predominance of Mexican news in "Noticiero" is a clear reflection of the audience, which network research shows to be about two-thirds Mexican and Mexican-American.

After Hallmark bought the network from Televisa, the most notable changes centered around coverage of Mexico. Televisa permitted no criticism of the Mexican government and its ruling party, known by its Spanish initials PRI, in its newscasts in Mexico or in the United States. Under U.S. ownership, Univisión journalists, correspondent Bruno López in particular, became feisty critics in the U.S. journalistic tradition. There are numerous examples: a muckraking report on abuses in Mexican government psychiatric hospitals (May 28, 1992); a report on negligence by the government oil company PEMEX, contributing to explosions that killed over 200 people in Guadalajara (April 12, 1992); a report questioning whether the government's pledge to privatize its broadcast companies and modernize its dealings with the media (by prohibiting government officials from bribing journalists) would substantively change Mexican political discourse (April 3, 1992).

Most significant was Univisión's reporting on Mexican electoral fraud. For example, in the summer of 1992, supporters of an opposition gubernatorial candidate in the state of Michoacán charged that the government's candidate had stolen the election. Univisión reported the fraud charges and then followed the story as the popular protests grew and the government's candidate was sworn in by the Mexican president. This only further invigorated the protesters, who, in a remarkable show of strength, marched several hundred miles to Mexico City. The crafting of these "Noticiero" stories was not remarkable; they were presented in completely straightforward and "balanced" ways. What made them extraordinary is that they were produced at all and broadcast in Mexico (albeit only on a relatively small cable system) and in the United States. [See chapter in this volume by Bruno López.]

"Noticiero Univisión" is both a reflection of and a model for U.S. Latino political culture. The journalists' voices, at once objective and enthusiastic in their affirmation of U.S. Latino cultures, are legitimating the use of the Spanish language as a language of U.S. political discourse. The Spanish language is the broadest, most encompassing symbol in the Univisión symbol system. Does that make the "Noticiero" just another national U.S. newscast but in Spanish? Yes and no.

It *is* just another U.S. national newscast, covering many of the same stories as ABC's "World News Tonight" and, as the analysis of the format of "Noticiero" has shown, in much the same style. The major divergence in *form* between ABC news and Univisión news is the Spanish language — a key indicator of the profoundly different journalistic mappings of the United States and the world that the two national news organizations have constructed.

Language, global maps and a special relationship to the audience all make "Noticiero Univisión" a distinctive presence in U.S. journalism and a key cultural resource for U.S. Latinos. However, it is important to note that for all these profound differences, there are also equally profound similarities between Univisión journalists and ABC journalists. They are all members of the same U.S. national news culture and commercial broadcasting industry; theirs is a U.S. cultural narrative. Univisión's U.S.-produced entertainment programs are modeled on successful mainstream programs. Similarly, Univisión journalists are practitioners of the U.S. professional journalistic ideology commonly referred to as "objectivity." This defining commonality with mainstream U.S. journalism creates the necessary professional space for Univisión journalists to report on such non-mainstream topics as U.S. Latino communities and Latin America.

"Noticiero" journalists understand their audience to be a community seeking a just and secure place *within* U.S. culture. To borrow Raymond Williams' typology, "Noticiero Univisión's" imagined community is not oppositional relative to mainstream U.S. political culture but alternative. Williams distinguishes between someone who finds a different way to live and wants to be left alone and someone who finds a different way to live and wants to use it to change society. As he acknowledged, the line between "alternative" and "oppositional" is a narrow one. In the case of "Noticiero Univisión's" imagined community, the audience is seen as one that wants to share in the riches of the American dream and participate in U.S. democracy while preserving and expressing distinctive Latino cultural attributes, particularly the Spanish language. It is a testament to the resiliency of the "melting pot" myth of U.S. immigration that this desire for cultural diversity within the United States is seen by some as an oppositional threat to U.S. civic culture.

The Return of Televisa USA

Recent developments in the ownership and corporate organization of Univisión raise doubts about the ability of the U.S. marketplace to sustain U.S.-produced, culturally diverse television programming. The last story of "Noticiero" on December 17, 1992, was brief and delivered in a studied monotone:

> Today the sale of Univisión to a group of investors led by Jerry Perenchio was finalized. Other participants are Televisa of Mexico and Venevisión of Venezuela. Perenchio announced today the conclusion of negotiations with Hallmark, which has been the owner of Univisión. In an announcement to employees, Perenchio said that as of now, he will be participating in decisions to assure the economic growth of Univisión and to maintain the commitments to the communities which it serves.

The sale of Univisión brought U.S. Spanish-language television full circle; the six-year Hallmark ownership became a brief pause in the 33-year domination of U.S. Spanish-language television by the Mexican entertainment conglomerate, Televisa.[7]

Televisa and Venevisión are minority partners, each owning 25 percent of the network. However, since Televisa is the largest producer of Spanish-language television programming in the world and is now co-owner of Panamsat, a Westar satellite used to distribute Univisión programming throughout the hemisphere,[8] it is quite feasible and economically rational for

Televisa once again to exert its controlling interest in Univisión. Within weeks of the sale, about 20 percent of Univisión's employees were laid off. The news department was particularly hard hit: the weekend editions of "Noticiero" were canceled, as was the weekly newsmagazine "Portada," despite its ratings ranking as the tenth most-watched program on U.S. Spanish-language television.[9] In addition, news bureaus in Brazil, Argentina and Chile were closed and field producers in the network's domestic bureaus laid off. The network's production facilities in Miami are currently for sale.

The sale to Azcárraga et al. has "Noticiero" journalists worried about censorship, especially in reporting from Mexico. Judging from Televisa's history, these are reasonable concerns. As of this writing, pressures to curb criticism of the Mexican government and the PRI are subtle and not clearly evident in the newscast. [See López in this volume.] All Univisión correspondents in Latin America are now required to assemble and transmit their stories from Televisa facilities. Under these arrangements, "Noticiero" stories from Mexico City-based correspondents could easily be physically censored. That crude form of censorship is not likely to be employed during a period when the Mexican government is intent on "modernizing" the country's media. Rather, Univisión journalists point to the diffuse "chilling effect" of working for Televisa, a company long known as the Ministry of Culture for the ruling Mexican political party, the PRI. The reductions in resources allotted to news production are having an effect on Univisión's journalistic credibility. The cancellation of "Portada" deprives journalists of an outlet for more detailed, thoughtful reporting.

The larger issue raised by the sale of Univisión is whether the U.S. market can sustain U.S.-produced television diversity. History tells us that without Emilio Azcárraga's deep pockets or, more precisely, the deep shelves of Televisa-produced programming, U.S. Spanish-language television would not exist. Producing television in the United States is considerably more expensive than importing it from Mexico. As one long-time observer of the industry, Félix Gutiérrez, puts it so well, it is good business to produce programming in *pesos* and sell it in dollars. This defining maxim of U.S. Spanish-language television applies equally to all programming, including the news.

Notes

1. The journalists who resigned formed the Hispanic Broadcasting Company, soon to become Telemundo, which today is the second-largest U.S. Spanish-language television network. About half of the remaining SIN journalists were kept on by the new Hallmark-owned Univisión, which was created in the months following the Zabludovsky affair.

2. The vice president for Univisión is Cuban-American, as are one of the co-executive producers of "Noticiero" and two of four Washington-based correspondents. The two co-anchors, as well as six U.S.-based correspondents, are Mexican-American. The weekend anchor and the national assignment editor are Puerto Rican. (Other staffers are natives or descendants of natives of other South American countries.)

3. This analysis is based on an examination of 375 Univisión stories and 407 ABC stories that aired on 25 alternate weekdays in May 1991 and June 1992.

4. The following analysis is drawn from the first stories of 50 newscasts: 25 "World News Tonight" and 25 "Noticiero Univisión."

5. The content analysis findings about the national origin of Univisión's U.S. Latino news makers are uncomfortably subjective; they were based on my coding of the particular Spanish-language accent and, so, national origin of the speaker.

6. The content analysis shows that ABC's "World News Tonight" gave 1.2 percent of its air time to U.S. Latino stories.

7. Telemundo, the second-largest U.S. Spanish-language television network, remains in precarious financial condition. On June 9, 1993, it declared bankruptcy but will remain on the air indefinitely. Its new strategy is to produce Spanish-language programming in the United States that is geared toward the Latin American export market. Galavisión, Televisa's premium U.S. cable-television network, is expected to be folded into Univisión.

8. Emilio Azcárraga's partner in Panamsat is René Anselmo, the former president of the Spanish International Network (SIN).

9. Other U.S.-produced programming was canceled as well, and according to Univisión staffers, the future of those remaining is not particularly bright.

Chapter 7

Balancing Act:
SURVIVING AS A TELEVISION
REPORTER IN MEXICO

Bruno López

The 1994 New Year's uprising in Chiapas caught the Mexican government and its press offices completely off guard. Hundreds of reporters arrived in the southern state of Chiapas days before any official spokespeople appeared on the scene. The Salinas cabinet couldn't decide whether to respond with diplomacy or with force. The national and foreign press were competing head-to-head on a fast-breaking story that was beyond the government's control.

In a country where news is usually tightly managed, the Chiapas rebellion offered an unusual opportunity for the Mexican media to show their true mettle. Several leading newspapers rose to the challenge, reporting independently and voluminously as the remarkable events unfolded. But Mexican television mostly clung to its habits of pro-government editorializing and self-censorship.

As a Mexican television journalist reporting for a U.S.-based Spanish-language news network, Univisión, I had an unusual vantage point, both as a close observer of Mexican television news and as an involuntary participant in its selective use of information and video from the field. My crew and I were among the first journalists to reach Ocosingo, a small highlands village that had been occupied by the guerrilla forces of the Zapatista National Liberation Army

Bruno López is the Mexico City bureau chief for Univisión. He previously worked as a broadcast journalist for Telemundo and CNN and as a print reporter for UPI and The Arizona Republic.

(Ejército Zapatista de Liberación Nacional — EZLN). On January 4, I filmed an interview with a Zapatista who had been shot during an exchange of gunfire with the military. He was obviously still in great pain. He claimed to have been forcibly recruited by the rebels and was on his way to work in the cornfields when the Zapatistas approached him and said, "The war has started; you're coming with us." He said that when he got to Ocosingo and saw that the Zapatistas had few weapons to distribute, he "knew he was going to die."

I included the interview in a piece I transmitted to Univisión's headquarters in Miami and to Televisa, the private near-monopoly Mexican television network. Televisa had recently become a minority equity partner in Univisión and was using Univisión material in its own newscasts.

My report included well-documented information about violations of human rights by Mexican security forces. We had grim footage of slain rebels lying in the dust in the Ocosingo market, their hands tied behind their backs — victims of summary military executions. But Mexican television viewers didn't see any of that. Televisa broadcast only my interview with the wounded man — the segment of the report that was most critical of the rebels.

The Zapatistas, for their part, made Mexican television one of their special targets. They excoriated Televisa's pro-government newscasts as an integral part of the "antidemocratic" system they were vowing to overthrow. They demanded that the government open up television news to their views and those of the opposition political parties. Practicing their own brand of censorship, rebel leaders banned Televisa cameras from their news conferences.

As a correspondent for a foreign network, I had been accustomed to reasonably open access to both the government and its opponents. But Televisa was able to use my Chiapas coverage in such a way that my independence was questioned. I ended up being distrusted by both sides — by the Zapatistas and their sympathizers, who thought we were too close to Televisa, and by the military and the Salinas administration, who thought we weren't nearly close enough.

On January 5, we traveled farther into Zapatista territory. The previous day, the army had been firing rockets at the area; several people had been killed, and we wanted to get the story. At first, the army wouldn't let us through. Then a tank came by with someone who seemed to be a senior officer. The soldiers asked him if we could enter. He looked at us and then signaled as if to say, "OK, let them through." I couldn't see him, but you could see that he had moved his hand and they let us through. I met up with Lucia Newmann, a Cable News Network (CNN) correspondent, who had managed to enter the area from the other side. She told me that everyone had left, except for one family; if we hurried, we would find them. We continued driving until we saw a little hut, parked the van and got out.

There was a white flag attached to our camera and a white T-shirt flapping from our boom mike. The roof of the van was marked "TV" in huge letters, and we had written "TV" across our windshield with masking tape. We started to walk, and the family started to approach us. Then I saw a Mexican air force plane overhead — and they began shooting directly at us! I didn't believe it at first. Then I noticed little mounds of sand flying into the air. We ran to take cover behind the rocks and stayed there for about 25 minutes. The plane passed by six or seven times, strafing the ground around us. The noise was deafening. We filmed the attack, and the video makes it clear that we were the intended targets.

That night the army issued a communiqué accusing us of having acted irresponsibly by entering a "prohibited zone," even though we had been waved through the military outpost. I later saw the army log of the day's activities: the attack on our crew was duly entered as a "pursuit of malefactors."

I edited the piece so that it wouldn't come across as an ego trip; I didn't want to air a "López under fire" story. Nor did I want to imply that this was a deliberate attempt by the military to intimidate the press, since we didn't know if the pilot was acting under orders. Instead, the story referred to the incident as one of several instances when the army appeared to have needlessly endangered civilians. I had local Catholic Church observers commenting that the extreme nervousness and lack of training apparent in army ranks had led to human rights abuses. I included a CNN video from Newmann, who had managed to talk to the family we had set out to interview. They said the army had been launching rockets in the area long after the Zapatistas left.

Univisión ran my story as I had sent it. Televisa ran the story after cutting out most of the strafing footage and all of my script. They ran a segment of our video showing the planes overhead while an announcer read the text of an army communiqué blaming *us* for allegedly provoking the attack.

We ran into a similar problem with another part of the Chiapas story. The Zapatistas had kidnapped a former Chiapas governor, Absalón González, whose administration had been notorious for persecuting Indian dissidents and for siding with powerful ranching families in local land tenure disputes. I bought video footage from a San Cristóbal free-lancer of an interview with González when the former governor was still a hostage and included it in a story reporting that he would soon be released. Televisa used the interview with the captive governor but not the rest of my file — nothing about González's political history, nothing about the rebels' motives for the kidnapping. All of this made it difficult for me to work in Chiapas because the Zapatistas saw me as an adjunct to Televisa.

When peace talks began in Chiapas a few weeks later, we had to fight for access to the EZLN and its charismatic leader, Subcomandante Marcos. We were kicked out of one interview that had been arranged for four or five TV crews. The Zapatistas said they didn't want to appear before our cameras because our cameras were the same as Televisa's cameras. We finally were granted a 20-minute interview with Marcos on the last day of the negotiations, in response to a letter from my producer saying that as an Indian he had been discriminated against all his life and it would be the height of irony if someone who claimed to be fighting on behalf of indigenous people also discriminated against him.

Coverage of the Chiapas uprising by print reporters in Mexico was more extensive, independent and probing than coverage on radio and television. Yet the broadcast media became increasingly bold as the story unfolded. Radio reporters gave live updates from the negotiations, including lengthy statements from Marcos and other rebel spokesmen. A few local TV outlets followed suit.

Even Televisa on several occasions gave Marcos more than five minutes of uninterrupted air time. Though his pronouncements had been front-page news across the country for weeks, it was the first time that a national television audience had heard his acerbic attacks on the Salinas government and the entire Mexican political system. (Still banned from EZLN briefings, Televisa bought its Marcos footage from a Chiapas affiliate.) It seemed unthinkable: a network that wouldn't usually broadcast the mildest criticism of the ruling party was turning its mikes over to a rifle-brandishing advocate of armed revolution. Why the sudden change? In part, Televisa producers probably felt protected because the negotiations they were covering had been ordered by President Salinas himself — and, presumably, no senior official told them *not* to put Marcos on the air.

More important, though, was the unaccustomed pressure of competition. This was the biggest breaking news story in Mexico in years, and Televisa, because of its own self-censorship, was being scooped by local and foreign news programs carried on cable and satellite systems in dozens of its major markets. Univisión's Miami-based nightly news show was now being seen on cable in more than 100 Mexican cities. Its main U.S. competition, Telemundo, also headquartered in Miami, was also available through cable or satellite dish in the major urban markets. A newly privatized national VHF network, Televisión Azteca, was broadcasting its own nightly news show. Just a few years back, Televisa and its cable subsidiaries had controlled virtually all news programming in Mexico. While Televisa's three channels still commanded a huge 90 percent of the national television audience, the company no longer had a de facto monopoly on news coverage. And Marcos was good for ratings: while Televisa carefully limited the rebel spokesman's appearances in its broadcasts for the first weeks of the uprising, every non-Televisa newscast was registering record audiences.

Still, Televisa's Chiapas coverage continued to emphasize the statements of government officials, while most Mexican print reporters were focusing on the poverty and discrimination and cynicism about national politics that had led Maya Indian farmers to support the uprising. Televisa remained banned from Zapatista press conferences. So were several newspapers and magazines controlled by Televisa's owners. And when the Zapatistas learned about Univisión's economic ties to Televisa, we began getting kicked out of their assemblies, too. (In the most aggravating case, we were summarily refused entry to a rebel conclave in the jungle after getting accredited and traveling 25 grueling hours through the rain forest.)

The irony for those of us at Univisión is that we had been perceived as the most formidable of Televisa's rivals — until the network's American owners, the Hallmark group, sold their holdings in 1992 to a consortium partially controlled by Televisa. Before the sale, we had felt that we were almost singlehandedly trying to open up Mexican television news to real independence and competition. When we first began to produce a national newscast in Spanish for the U.S. market, it was also broadcast in Mexico City by the local cable system Multivisión, the rival of the larger, Televisa-controlled Cablevisión system. Later, our "Noticiero Univisión" nightly news show was aired on VHF stations in Veracruz, Hermosillo, and — in a real coup — Guadalajara, the country's second-biggest city. Ratings in Guadalajara in the summer of 1991 showed "Noticiero Univisión" soundly trouncing "24 Horas," Televisa's nightly newscast, our own ratings information showed. Univisión's owners began contemplating a bid for the state television network that was being privatized by the Salinas government, a move that would have put us into head-to-head competition with "24 Horas" across the country.

That never happened. Instead, in April 1992, Hallmark sold Univisión to a consortium led by A. Jerrold Perenchio, a Hollywood television producer, with Televisa and Venevisión of Caracas as minority partners. The Mexican and Venezuelan shareholders together bought the maximum 20-percent stake permitted foreign investors under U.S. Federal Communications Commission (FCC) television network ownership rules. Given Televisa's cozy relationship with the Mexican government, I feared that someone there might try to have me removed from my Univisión post or would at least complain about my coverage to the Univisión management in Miami. To my surprise, I haven't experienced any editorial interference, and we have a good working relationship with Televisa in Mexico City: we get access to video footage that I wouldn't otherwise have, and we are able to use Televisa's facilities to send feeds from remote locations like Chiapas.

Still, Televisa continues to use our pieces in partial or distorted form, and Univisión's business relationship with Televisa means that we are no longer perceived to be completely independent. Crowds at news events in Mexico are often openly abusive toward Televisa crews, and we had felt some of that same hostility even before the Univisión-Televisa partnership. This tension was especially acute at opposition rallies during hard-fought local elections that rarely receive balanced coverage on national news shows. When we were covering state elections in San Luis Potosí, our crew was often greeted by chants of "Prensa local, vergüenza nacional"("Local press, national shame"). We defended ourselves by stressing that we worked for Univisión, a network based in Miami — "It's foreign, uncensored and uncontrolled." For our own safety, it was crucial to avoid being confused with Televisa; during previous state elections in Tamaulipas, a Televisa cameraman was severely beaten by a youthful mob of opposition supporters. Televisa's cameramen are now so fearful of being attacked that they often refuse to wear the company's distinctive yellow jackets.

In areas where Univisión is readily available, we can usually count on a friendly reception. In a 1994 PRI campaign rally in Tijuana, for example, where our program is widely viewed, a group of onlookers greeted us with chants of "Long Live Univisión! Death to Televisa!" Elsewhere, however, people we interview often spontaneously censor themselves in a way that they would not if they were speaking to foreign reporters. We reassure them that we are an independent international news network and that they are free to say whatever they want. Some people respond with immediate frankness; they light up as if the very idea of uncensored news were a revelation. Others persist in answering in the most diplomatic and convoluted manner possible. "I'm trying to sound low-key and unthreatening so that you can use it," a Mexico City economist once said to me after a cautiously ambivalent on-air interview.

Until 1993, we fed our stories from a place known by TV people here as "the second floor" — a transmission room in a government telecommunications complex. The video transmission plays over a monitor in the office as the signal is relayed to a control room on the top of the building and from there via an earth station to the satellite. The transmission office is the only office in the building run directly by the Ministry of Internal Affairs, which is responsible for internal security and political surveillance as well as radio and television licensing. In theory, the ministry has the ability and authority to censor outgoing video transmissions, though it rarely exercises that power. We transmitted our stories from the second-floor office as often as three times a week. Our reports frequently documented instances of government corruption and included interviews with government critics who are rarely seen on local television. The government technicians would ask in amazement if we were "authorized" to transmit these stories. We always assured them that we were.

Sometimes, however, the Ministry of Internal Affairs has attempted to control our coverage — especially when it involved the Ministry itself. In August 1993, we were working on a story on radio censorship. Six radio journalists had been fired by stations around the country. Their station managers claimed privately that the Ministry of Internal Affairs had ordered them to do so in an effort to rid the airwaves of critical commentary prior to the 1994 presidential campaign. The managers claimed that if they didn't bow to this pressure, their broadcasting licenses would be jeopardized. For a response, we called the head of the Ministry's Radio, Television and Film Office (Radio, Televisión y Cine — RTC), Mexico's equivalent of the FCC. The RTC director demanded that I first speak to him privately. I went to his office, where he vehemently denied the story, contending there was no organized censorship effort by Mexican authorities. He refused my request for an on-camera interview, citing what he contended was an antigovernment bias in my coverage of Mexico for Univisión. To document the charge, he took a stack of videocassettes from his bookcase. They were copies of my Univisión news feeds. "I am concerned," he said, gesturing at the tapes, "because I've noticed inaccuracy and slander here. And whether you like it or not, in Mexico the law is very clear. It establishes sanctions for things like this." The last part of this was true — there are draconian statutes on the books, giving the government great power to punish news organizations for broadcasting material deemed to be offensive or unpatriotic. He acknowledged that this power was rarely exercised, and then he leaned forward for greater emphasis. "But we have decided that it's time," he added, "to enforce the law regardless of the consequences."

He then abruptly changed his tone to that of a fatherly friend worried about my future. "You really have to be more careful," he advised. "You don't want people to think you are with the opposition. You see, you go out and interview all these critics of the government who speak irresponsibly on any subject." He then showed me a set of report cards his office had assembled on local and foreign media coverage, noting as either "positive" or "negative" all references to President Carlos Salinas, the ruling party, the government and the opposition. The clear message was that my coverage was being methodically monitored for political content and that reprisals for unfriendly reporting were under active consideration.

I came away feeling that I had better back up my radio censorship story with more corroborating evidence before I put it on the air. A few months later, another radio commentator was fired, and the station manager told the same story. I again called the RTC director, and he finally agreed to an on-camera interview. A few days later, he was removed from the post, allegedly because the president was embarrassed by the overzealousness of his media gatekeeper.

Most of the pressures we face are more subtle. Journalists known for openly critical reporting find that their requests for information and interviews are blocked by the president's press office. In a centralized political system like Mexico's, that can effectively block access to every government agency and ministry. President Salinas' first press secretary, Otto Granados, often phoned complaints about my stories to my bosses in Miami, questioning my integrity and professionalism. He would get particularly exercised by interviews with prominent left-of-center critics like Jorge Castañeda or Adolfo Aguilar Zínser, who were routinely quoted in foreign media but who almost never appeared on local television. Granados would tell my editors that Castañeda and Aguilar "lacked prestige" and were "uninformed" about the subject in question.

Univisión's executives ignored these complaints and encouraged me to continue my reporting, but this constant pressure is easier for editors in Miami to withstand than for editors, producers and publishers in Mexico City. The Mexican news media, especially the broadcast media, are used to a system where one political party has had control over licensing rules, tax policy, public advertising budgets and virtually all unionized employees and service personnel. Many owners of media companies are themselves part of the PRI elite. The result, all too often, is self-censorship, sometimes subtle, sometimes blatant. At Televisa, this instinct seems so deeply inculcated that there is little need for direct official pressure. Their producers and anchors often appear to see themselves not as journalists but as government spokespeople.

Yet, as was shown during the Chiapas rebellion and during the 1994 presidential election campaign, news organizations that report independently not only survive, they gain new readers and viewers. The anger of ordinary citizens about biased television coverage has already convinced many Televisa reporters that things have to change. If ratings show Televisa's market share eroding in major cities, maybe its executives will come around to the same point of view. The rest of us in the business would welcome the competition.

Section III

Attacking the Messenger

Chapter 8

From Intimidation to Assassination:
Silencing the Press

Lucy Conger

Journalism in Mexico can be a violent business. Reporters who expose official corruption or write detailed stories about drug trafficking can expect threats, physical attacks and sometimes even attempts on their lives. Some acts of violence against journalists come from criminal elements and local political factions; others have been directly attributable to federal police agencies. Over the past decade, the Mexican government has not only failed to shield journalists against these pressures, it has abdicated its responsibility to investigate these abuses vigorously and prosecute whoever is found responsible.

How serious is the problem? One way to evaluate it is simply to count the deaths of journalists who have been murdered because of their work. That is difficult, however. There are many different tallies, and documentation in many cases is contradictory or incomplete. The Mexico City-based National Center for Social Communication (Centro Nacional de Comunicación Social — CENCOS) reported that 35 Mexican journalists died violent deaths during the six years of the Carlos Salinas de Gortari administration. In the previous six years, under President Miguel de la Madrid Hurtado, there were more than 20 reported murders or suspicious accidental deaths of working reporters and editors, many of which appeared to be deliberate job-related homicides.

Lucy Conger reported on Mexico from 1984 to 1995 as a correspondent for Institutional Investor, Jornal do Brasil *and other publications. She is now a free-lance journalist in Philadelphia specializing in Latin American topics.*

In most of these cases — as in most homicides in Mexico — there has never been a prosecution or even a thorough investigation. Not all of these cases are necessarily related to journalism. The Committee to Protect Journalists (CPJ), using stricter criteria, was able to document probable links between these deaths and the victims' professional work as journalists in just nine of these cases. In another 11 cases documented by the CPJ of seemingly deliberate assassinations of journalists in that period, police investigations were contradictory or incomplete, and plausible motives for the killings included but were not limited to the victims' journalistic work. (In the first year of President Ernesto Zedillo's administration there was yet another case of a journalist's job-related murder.) Other international press freedom groups, such as the Inter American Press Association (IAPA), report similar findings. Yet even 10 confirmed assassinations of journalists in the course of a decade is a disturbingly large number — higher, in fact, than in any other nation in the hemisphere in that period, with the exception of Colombia. Some of these victims were major figures in local or national media. The Union of Democratic Journalists (Unión de Periodistas Democráticos — UPD) is still pressing for further investigations in four of the best-known and best-documented of these murders: the 1988 assassination of Héctor Félix "Gato" Miranda, co-editor of the Tijuana weekly newspaper *Zeta*; the 1988 murder of Manuel Burgueño Orduño, columnist for the Mazatlán daily, *El Sol del Pacífico*; the 1986 slayings of reporter Norma Alicia Moreno Figueroa and editor Ernesto Flores Torrijos of *El Popular,* a newspaper in Matamoros, Tamaulipas; and the 1984 murder of the nationally syndicated *Excélsior* columnist Manuel Buendía Tellezgirón. Reports of assaults on journalists are also disturbingly frequent: CENCOS counted more than 200 such cases in the 15-year period between 1971 and 1986. There are also many incidents of journalists being arbitrarily detained by police and threatened by local civil and police officials.

Soon after its creation in 1990, the government-sponsored National Human Rights Commission (Comisión Nacional de Derechos Humanos — CNDH) initiated a special program to investigate 55 cases of attacks on and killings of journalists, beginning with a list of cases presented by the Union of Democratic Journalists. The 55 cases included 43 attacks on or killings of newspaper and magazine reporters and editors. The other 12 cases included two radio reporters, one television reporter, two family members killed with journalists and seven people who were non-reporting employees of the media or had been incorrectly identified as journalists. Two years later, the Commission had completed investigations in 40 of those cases. It concluded that many appeared to be unrelated to journalism but called for further investigations — investigations that were never carried out. The CNDH confirmed that 22 journalists had been murdered, all but one outside Mexico City; it was either unable or did not attempt to determine who was responsible for these deaths or what their motives might have been.

As the statistics demonstrate, the risks in the profession increase with distance from Mexico City. Isolation from the capital leaves provincial reporters without the protective shield provided by contacts and friendships with national and foreign reporters. In local jurisdictions, says Jesús Cantú, editorial director of *El Noroeste* of Culiacán, Sinaloa, "governors and *caciques* operate by the law of the jungle." Mexico City political columnist Carlos Ramírez notes that provincial reporters are often victimized by the dependency of their newspapers on advertising and other favors from state governors' offices. The intimidation or harassment of local reporters and editors usually originates locally, not at the national or federal level, Mexican political analysts say. However, as with other types of violations, attacks on the provincial news media are thought to proliferate because state and local authorities act on their belief that these violations will be tolerated by the central government.

Press Policy Under Salinas

President Salinas can be credited with loosening state controls over the press and for tolerating — though not actively encouraging — the increasing editorial independence of leading newspapers in major cities. The Salinas government ended the state monopoly on the production and importation of newsprint, stopped paying all travel expenses for reporters covering the president's foreign travels and issued guidelines "strictly prohibiting" federal agencies from giving money or favors to any journalists.

But Salinas also presided over a period characterized by renewed attacks on journalists and continued restriction and manipulation of public information. Attacks on provincial journalists and periodicals continued unabated. Thorough investigations into the murders of reporters were the exception to a general rule of impunity.

The murder of Víctor Manuel Oropeza is one case in point. In July 1991, Oropeza, a journalist, medical doctor and opposition activist, was brutally stabbed to death in his office. Oropeza was a homeopathic physician and columnist who wrote outspoken articles opposing election fraud and the alleged murders of Indian peasants by federal narcotics agents. He was also a high-profile participant in local protests against electoral fraud. Following a public outcry, two men were arrested, tried and convicted for the murder. The CNDH investigation found that the suspects had been tortured into confessing and recommended that the convictions be overturned. The two men were released. Several state judicial police officers were dismissed for their roles in framing the suspects. María Teresa Jardi, a prominent human rights lawyer who was then working as an adviser to federal Attorney General Ignacio Morales Lechuga, resigned her post in protest over the government's handling of the case.

More routine harassment of journalists rarely prompted even an investigation, much less a prosecution. A typical example was the series of attacks in the summer of 1992 on *El Diario de Yucatán,* the peninsula's leading independent daily. In July, the home of editor Carlos Menéndez was attacked by unidentified people who stood outside his house for 20 minutes, throwing stones and attempting to force open the front door. In August, a bomb was found at the newspaper office; it was successfully deactivated by a Mexican army bomb squad. No arrests were made following either incident. Menéndez considered these attacks reprisals for articles exposing the use of government-paid thugs to disrupt a protest demonstration of Maya Indian farmers in the Yucatán state capital.

Even the best-known journalists have experienced such harassment. Jorge G. Castañeda, a prominent author, government critic and newspaper columnist (and a contributor to this volume), received indirect death threats in June 1990 through his secretary, Mariana Rodríguez Villegas, who twice was terrorized by gun-toting men on a Mexico City street. Morales Lechuga, at the time attorney general for Mexico City, publicly attempted to discredit Rodríguez Villegas' account of the incidents. Public reaction to the incident led President Salinas to intervene directly, calling Castañeda to condemn the harassment and offer federal protection.

In an unprecedented move, media censorship came under official scrutiny in 1992 when the CNDH agreed to study a grievance filed by the Mexican Academy of Human Rights. The complainants, Sergio Aguayo Quezada and Oscar Ortiz, protested their being cut off the air in 1991 in the middle of a question-and-answer segment on state-owned television, Imevisión, in which the activists were explaining the objectives of the Academy's program to promote political rights. The talk show included a discussion of the Academy's activities organizing election observers to detect and prevent fraud in the sensitive San Luis Potosí gubernatorial election of August 18, 1991, where the PRI faced a respected independent challenger. In its first recommendation in a case of media censorship, the CNDH found the censorship was "without legal basis" and recommended that Imevisión investigate and discipline those employees responsible for interrupting the transmission and that it broadcast a complete interview with the complainants. Within weeks, the network had complied partially with the recommendation, airing the 1991 program that had been cut off. However, then-director of state-owned Imevisión, Romeo Flores Caballero, refused to investigate and discipline the public servants responsible for cutting off the program. "He (Flores Caballero) appears to be ignorant of the recommendation," Ortiz said in an interview.

Mexican journalists contend that despite such gestures, the Salinas government often used heavy-handed intimidation tactics to influence news coverage. On at least a few occasions, Salinas administration officials confiscated publications containing negative stories. The news weekly *Proceso,* which publishes long muckraking critiques of government policies and high officials, was one frequent target. In March 1990, local authorities in Guerrero stopped circulation of an issue of *Proceso* documenting official repression of opposition protests against electoral fraud in the state. Newsstand copies of the January 25, 1993, issue of the Spanish news weekly *Cambio 16* mysteriously vanished, according to the magazine's editors in Madrid; the issue featured a cover story on opposition leader Cuauhtémoc Cárdenas and his contention that relatives of President Salinas had profited from government privatization contracts.

The ruling Institutional Revolutionary Party (Partido Revolucionario Institucional — PRI) — under the president's direct command — used both bribery and its enormous advertising budget to assure positive news coverage, Mexican reporters charge. The entrenched local press tradition of selling front-page "news stories" to the highest bidder greatly facilitated such corruption. This was particularly notable in states where the Cárdenas-led Democratic Revolutionary Party (Partido de la Revolución Democrática — PRD) had a strong following. In 1992, Tabasco state government receipts showed that Governor Salvador Neme Castillo paid an average of $12,000 monthly to four local magazines to obtain favorable reporting, according to published reports.

There were other less direct pressures on independent journalists. Under Salinas, as under previous administrations, the illegal government wiretapping of telephone lines was assumed to be a fact of life by independent reporters and editors, just as it is for opposition activists. "Of course they tap our telephones; those are the rules of the game," says Sergio Aguayo, director of the private Mexican Academy of Human Rights. This supersedes paranoia: transcripts of the conversations between officials and reporters occasionally surface in newspaper offices.

Police Corruption and Abuse of the Press

As in Colombia, many of the murders of reporters in Mexico can be attributed to the corrupt nexus of drug traffickers and their agents and protectors in national security forces and in the highest spheres of civilian government.

The most notorious and still the most important of these cases was the May 30, 1984, killing of nationally known *Excélsior* columnist Manuel Buendía. At the time, it was widely rumored that he had been murdered to stop a planned exposé on ties between drug traffickers and powerful figures in the cabinet of President Miguel de la Madrid Hurtado. It was not until five years later, though, that the government took serious steps toward resolving the case. On June 13, 1989, José Antonio Zorrilla Pérez was arrested following a gun battle in Mexico City and charged with ordering Buendía's murder. At the time of Buendía's murder, Zorrilla had been the director of the Federal Security Directorate (Directorio Federal de Seguridad — DFS), a powerful and thoroughly corrupt plainclothes police agency that was charged with monitoring the political opposition and overseeing the prosecution of drug traffickers. He had also been a personal friend and source of Buendía and had arrived at the scene of the killing 20 minutes after it occurred.

Zorrilla was held in the Reclusorio Norte of Mexico City for three years and eight months before being sentenced on February 15, 1993, to 35 years in jail for conspiracy to commit murder. Zorrilla was accused of removing from Buendía's office files that Buendía kept on numerous sensitive topics, including the DFS itself. Three other former DFS commanders and one former agent were also sentenced in the crime. A young man named Juan Rafael Moro Avila was identified as the actual assassin.

On January 13, 1990, in Mexico City, Felipe Victoria Cepeda, a journalist and author of a book on the death of Manuel Buendía, was detained by 30 antinarcotics agents of the Federal Judicial Police (Policía Judicial Federal — PJF) as he approached the federal attorney general's office headquarters to obtain information about a story. Victoria Cepeda said he was handcuffed, kicked, hit in the stomach and dragged into the building where he was held incommunicado for several days and threatened with death.

Other murders were also linked to coverage of police involvement in drug trafficking. On February 22, 1988, Manuel Burgueño Orduño, a columnist for the Mazatlán daily *El Sol del Pacífico*, was shot to death in his home. Burgueño frequently wrote about the alleged ties between local and state officials and drug traffickers. Two men were sentenced to more than 31 years in prison for the murder, and a third suspect escaped from jail during the trial. The UPD does not consider the case closed, however, and told the CNDH it would present evidence regarding a presumed mastermind.

On April 20, 1988, Héctor Félix "Gato" (or Felix the Cat) Miranda, columnist and co-editor of the weekly *Zeta* in Tijuana, Baja California, was shot to death as he drove on a Tijuana street. Miranda was a nationally known humorist who regularly satirized the corrupt practices of local and state officials in his column. One favorite target was Tijuana race track owner Jorge Hank Rhon, son of the current Minister of Agriculture, Carlos Hank González. Authorities arrested Victoriano Medina Moreno, a security guard at Hank Rhon's race track, and said he had confessed to the murder. In court, however, Medina proclaimed his innocence and said he had been tortured into confessing. Authorities also arrested another race track employee, Antonio Vera Palestina, in the murder. Medina and Vera Palestina were sentenced to 27 and 25 years, respectively. Their motive was never clarified in the proceedings, however. The UPD has asked the CNDH to keep the case open until the author of the crime has also been identified and prosecuted.

Intimidation in the Context of Political Conflict

While there have been no documented instances of journalists being killed for reporting on political tensions, there have been a number of accounts of intimidation of journalists, particularly from the states of Michoacán and Guerrero following hotly contested state and local elections. In one case, Sara Lovera, a *La Jornada* reporter covering post-election violence in Guerrero, received veiled threats from Antorcha Campesina (Peasant Torch), a radical peasant organization with close ties to the PRI and a reputation for confrontation and violence. Accusations attempting to discredit Lovera appeared in an Antorcha-paid advertisement in *unomásuno* after Lovera reported that the municipality of Alcozauca, Guerrero, was under siege by 125 armed members of Antorcha Campesina who threatened the mayor and former mayor, both members of the PRD.

On March 22, 1990, soldiers at a teachers' demonstration in Uruapán, Michoacán, struck journalists with their weapons, apparently for having taken photographs of them. Three journalists were injured: Guillermo Cerda León, correspondent for *El Universal*; Gerardo Sánchez, a writer for the weekly *Imagen*; and Raúl Ramos, correspondent for *El Sol de Morelia*.

In October 1992, reporters from the state of Tabasco called on President Salinas to free José Angel Muñoz González, correspondent for the *Tabasco Hoy* newspaper. Muñoz González was being held in the Pichucalco jail in Chiapas under charges of participating in a public disturbance that resulted in the ouster of the mayor of the town of Reforma and the death of one person. Apprehended by judicial police, Muñoz González was accused of theft, damage to property and injury to others.

In April 1989, Audelino Macario, at the time Tabasco correspondent for *La Jornada*, was accused in the press by the state attorney general of inciting violence. Terrified, Macario filed for an *amparo*, or restraining order, to protect himself from arrest. The charges came in the wake of Macario's coverage of the growing strength of the PRD and post-election violence in the town of San Carlos.

Press Intimidation for Other Reasons

It is a long-standing practice for Mexican officials to use official favors, state advertising budgets and access to information to reward or punish the news media. Direct cash payments to favored reporters and editors are also routine. Publishers of pro-government newspapers — which is to say, most newspapers — have often fired reporters in direct response to official complaints about corruption stories or uncritical coverage of the opposition. These practices, though often difficult to document, were common at all levels of the Salinas administration, knowledgeable journalists concur. The biggest taboo for Mexican newspapers, as always, was unfriendly coverage of the president, the president's family and the inner circle of his top advisers.

On November 25, 1991, the editor-in-chief of the Monterrey newspaper *El Porvenir* resigned, alleging that he had been forced out as a result of pressure on the publisher from President Salinas' office. The editor, Jesús Cantú, said he was told that the president's office was angry at what it perceived to be disrespectful coverage of the president. Cantú cited a campaign of mounting pressure that began in May 1989 with a meeting with Salinas' chief spokesman, Otto Granados, who allegedly warned him: "I'll tell you the rules for operating: these are respect for the president, respect for the presidential image and professional work. These are sensible, rational rules ... but if you want others, we can also work with those." In his resignation letter, Cantú said that following the meeting with Granados, the government refused to issue press credentials to his reporters and canceled all state advertising contracts. He further charged that government officials had conspired successfully to have him removed from his job.

In 1991, *Excélsior* columnist Manú Dornbierer published accusations that two brothers of President Salinas, Raúl and Enrique Salinas, were rumored to have acquired 50-percent ownership of a Mexico City race track. The story was vigorously denied in letters to the editor from Mexico City Attorney General Morales Lechuga and Justo Fernández, concessionaire of the race track. *Excélsior*, a paper that has closely reflected government thinking for a long time in its news columns and on its editorial page, refused to publish a column Dornbierer wrote in response to the letters. She resigned from the paper, saying, "During the three years and some remaining to Salinas in the presidency, it is obvious that I cannot work with liberty and safety."

In November 1992, Zachary Margulis, an American reporter for Mexico City's English-language daily *The News*, was dismissed after publishing an op-ed article in *The New York Times* denouncing constraints on press freedom in Mexico. Margulis recounted the quashing of a story he had written "based on a U.S. Drug Enforcement Administration report in which a DEA informant linked Manuel Bartlett Díaz ... to the murder of a Veracruz journalist." Bartlett Díaz, who served in the cabinets of both the de la Madrid and Salinas administrations, was the PRI candidate for governor of Puebla at the time Margulis filed his story for *The News*.

Continuing Impunity

E ven when the government initially responds to the murders of journalists, investigators often quietly abandon the cases weeks or months later.

One such case is that of Odilón López Urías, who as editor of the *Onda* newspaper of Sinaloa had attacked drug traffickers and corruption among local officials in his paper. On October 7, 1986, while driving with his family, he was kidnapped by more than six armed men who, witnesses said, appeared to be government officials or police officers. López Urías' body was found a few days later. The CNDH investigated the case and sent a recommendation to the governor of Sinaloa on May 14, 1991. The Commission found that the last inquiry made into the case by investigating officers was on May 11, 1988. Although the case was not solved, the investigation stopped after public awareness of the case diminished.

The case of Emilio Santiago Alvarado, who was shot on March 6, 1985, while promoting the newspaper *Portavoz* over a portable microphone in Tehuacán, Puebla, is similar. Santiago Alvarado had formerly been a critic of local government and of corruption in big business. On April 30, 1991, the CNDH issued a recommendation in the case and noted that no investigative work had been done since April 30, 1985. The CNDH pointed out that many leads existed in the case that had not been examined.

The failure to investigate thoroughly the 1988 murder of Héctor "Félix the Cat" Miranda in Tijuana typifies the approach taken in cases that might implicate powerful people. Years later, the Tijuana weekly *Zeta* is still pressing for a full investigation of the murder of its star columnist. The editors of *Zeta* insist that the government should question Jorge Hank Rhon, son of Salinas' powerful agriculture minister, and Hank Rhon's friend, Alberto Murjía. They have also demanded testimony from six judicial police officers involved in the case and from the PRI's former gubernatorial candidate, Margarita Ortega Villa.

With President Ernesto Zedillo promising that "nobody is above the law," some of these cases may yet be revisited by federal authorities. If there are serious investigative efforts, they would send a needed message to Mexican journalists that their intimidators are no longer untouchable. But if the government fails to pursue and punish those responsible for these crimes, regardless of their financial power or political connections, Mexico will never enjoy a truly free and independent press.

Chapter 9

Mexican News and American Diplomacy:
U.S. State Department Monitoring of Press Freedom Violations in Mexico

Mary C. Moynihan

In keeping with its legislative mandate to report on "internationally recognized human rights,"[1] the U.S. State Department has addressed "Freedom of Speech and Press"[2] in its reports on Mexico since 1977. The Department of State reports have documented a continuing pattern of noncompliance in Mexico with the basic tenets of a free press. The reports record numerous instances of violence against journalists perpetrated by individuals in power, in retaliation or as a means of discouraging reportage of controversial events. Indeed, the reports document the murders of at least 15 people in Mexico since 1977 in circumstances that directly point to press freedom issues. In addition, the reports detail the subtler means by which the Mexican government has exerted influence over the press.

The reports have been issued every year since 1977, when the U.S. Congress first required the U.S. Department of State to produce reports on the status of human rights in all countries that receive aid from the United States and all countries that are members of the United Nations.[3] For the past several years, the State Department has also produced reports on the few countries that are not covered by the congressional requirement. These Department of State Reports on Human Rights Practices have developed into an important tool in evaluating human rights performance throughout the world.

Mary C. Moynihan is an associate with the New York law office of Sullivan and Cromwell. She also has worked with The Lawyers Committee for Human Rights.

While the reports suffer in certain instances from administration biases and in some cases lack of thoroughness, by the State Department's own account the reports "have increasingly become the standard reference source for information on human rights for users both in and out of government and a major element in U.S. human rights policy."[4] The reports are based upon all information available to the U.S. government, including that from American officials, officials of foreign governments, private citizens, victims of human rights abuses, congressional studies, intelligence information, press reports, international organizations and non-governmental organizations concerned with human rights.

Unfortunately, although coverage in the State Department reports of freedom of the press has improved somewhat over the years, early coverage tended to be sparse and lacking in serious analysis. For example, reports in the late 1970s noted that direct criticism of the incumbent president was muted and generally avoided but otherwise concluded that the media had conducted a full national debate. In addition, the reports have often repeated intact whole portions of text from the previous year's report, suggesting little if any original research. This is particularly egregious where easily available press and media reports, as well as findings by non-governmental human rights monitoring organizations, have documented matters not covered or inaccurately reported in the relevant State Department report. The most serious flaws in the reports, however, have been their failure to provide detailed background information with respect to the incidents they have reported and failure to provide follow-up information in subsequent reports regarding arrests of the perpetrators or other resolutions of those incidents.

Violence Against Journalists

The State Department first focused attention on violence against journalists in its report for 1986. The report recounted that during that year several journalists died violently or under suspicious circumstances and that retaliation for coverage of local problems may have been a motive. In particular, the 1986 report discussed the murders of José Luis Nava Linda, Ernesto Flores Torrijos and Norma Alicia Moreno Figueroa, Odilón López Urías, Carlos Loret de Mola and Jorge Brenes.

Nava, who was the editor of the Guerrero periodical *Expresión Popular*, was killed (allegedly assassinated) in May 1986 shortly after running a series of articles against the Institutional Revolutionary Party (Partido Revolucionario Institucional — PRI). According to the report, court records indicated he had quarreled with another man, Javier Ibáñez, and that he was shot when attempting to draw his own gun on Ibáñez. Ibáñez was arrested for homicide in June, and an interim prison sentence was handed down in July. He appealed his conviction, and the sentence was revoked in August.

Flores and Moreno were editor and reporter, respectively, for the newspaper *El Popular*. According to the report, they were killed by unknown gunmen in July 1986 in Matamoros, Tamaulipas. *El Popular* was noted for its highly personal but apparently well-documented attacks on local officials. The Federal Judicial Police (Policía Judicial Federal — PJF) commenced an investigation, but no resolution had been reached at the time of the 1986 report.

Also in 1986, Sinaloa reporter and columnist López was found dead after having been kidnapped two days before by eight armed men, according to the report. López was well known in Sinaloa for his reporting on drug and criminal figures in the state and for his contentions that government figures were involved in drug trafficking.

Loret de Mola was former governor of Guerrero and a political columnist for the newspaper *Excélsior*. He died in an automobile accident in the state of Guerrero, apparently when his car went over a cliff on a dangerous stretch of highway. As a result of anomalies in the chronology of events, however, the report noted, there were doubts as to whether he actually died in the accident or it was staged after his death.

Finally, the 1986 report recounted that Brenes, a newspaper publisher in Reynosa, was killed in July by two men. The report stated that the motive was unknown, but there was speculation that the murderers were hired.

Subsequent reports have made no further mention of the surrounding facts or the resolutions, if any, of any of these murders.

In its 1987 report, the U.S. State Department recounted that according to members of the media, several journalists had died violently or under suspicious circumstances in 1987 but that the report gave no details regarding the deaths. The report also stated that four assaults against journalists had been reported. In particular, Oscar Santiago Crisanti, a reporter for the newspaper *El Mundo de Tampico*, had been shot and severely wounded in March 1987, shortly after he had accused municipal police of having hired known criminals.

Again in 1988, the U.S. State Department reported that several journalists died violently or under suspicious circumstances in retaliation for coverage of local and national problems. According to the report, these incidents included the murder on April 20 of popular Tijuana investigative reporter Héctor Félix "El Gato" Miranda; the murder on February 22 of Mazatlán journalist, lawyer and university professor Manuel Burgueño Orduño; and an incident on July 15 that took the life of Ciudad Juárez television personality Linda Bejarano. The 1988 report gave no additional details about these deaths.[5]

The 1989 report, however, noted that the murder of Manuel Burgueño Orduño was solved, with no further elaboration. In addition, the 1990 report followed up with the information that a principal suspect in the assassination of Héctor Félix "El Gato" Miranda had been arrested in May of that year. This is in seeming contrast, however, to a statement in the 1989 report that the murder of Héctor Félix was solved in 1989. The 1992 report recounted that two men (neither of whom was a public servant) were convicted of the murder and sentenced to terms of 25 and 27 years but that the case was later reopened to consider new evidence. Finally, according to the 1990 report, the Mexican attorney general's office opened a new investigation in 1990 into the possible complicity of Joaquín Salvador Galván, an ex-commander of the Mexican PJF in Ciudad Juárez, in the murder of Linda Bejarano; subsequently, in its 1992 report, the State Department reported that six killers involved in the murder of National Action Party (Partido Acción Nacional — PAN) journalist Linda Bejarano had been sentenced to 25- to 27-year terms but implied that the murder was not politically motivated.

The 1989 report stated that no Mexican journalists were known to have died violently in 1989. However, it cited press reports that a reporter for *El Sol Veracruzano* was abducted in Mexico City in early January and that as many as nine press reporters were assaulted in 1989.

The 1989 report also stated that the murder of *Excélsior* journalist Manuel Buendía was purportedly solved after a five-year investigation. The reports had failed in previous years to mention Buendía's death, the ongoing investigation or the arrests. In fact, Buendía was killed May 30, 1984, under circumstances suggesting connections to the activities of the U.S. Drug Enforcement Administration.[6] According to the 1989 report, a police agent, Juan Rafael Moro Avila, was accused of the crime. Moro, in turn, blamed a former policeman for the actual murder and maintained that Antonio Zorrilla Pérez, a former chief of the Federal Security Directorate, an intelligence unit that was later dismantled, was the mastermind of the crime. In its 1990 report, the State Department reported that Moro was sentenced in April 1990 to one year in prison for arms possession and Zorrilla sentenced in September to a 30-year prison term for an unrelated murder. The 1991 report stated that the investigation of Buendía's murder remained pending because of Zorrilla's imprisonment on the murder charge.

In 1990, the report described the cases of several reporters who died violently or were wounded under suspicious circumstances. Alfredo Córdova Solórzano, a correspondent for *Excélsior,* was shot in Tapachula, Chiapas, in an incident that, according to the report, Chiapas Governor Patrocinio González Garrido later ruled accidental. In addition, three police officers were accused of the murder of *El Día* reporter Elvira Marcelo Esquival. A correspondent for *Excélsior* and director of the Tabasco weekly *El Fondo* was physically attacked after having received death threats, reportedly from a Tabasco state government representative to Mexico City. Finally, Mario Barajas Pérez, the editor of *El Sol de Morelia,* was reportedly detained and beaten by the PJF when he attempted to photograph an incident involving PJF officers.

The 1990 report also described an incident in which two building guards for the prominent Mexico City daily *La Jornada* were gunned down on April 12, purportedly by agents of the underground Clandestine Workers' Revolutionary Party Union. The former rector of the Benito Juárez Autonomous University of Oaxaca, Felipe Martínez Soriano, was accused by the federal district attorney of masterminding the attack. The report also states that several noted Mexican journalists and academics, among them Jorge Castañeda, Adolfo Aguilar Zínser and Lorenzo Meyer, repeatedly received death threats in June and that *La Jornada* founder Rodolfo Peña received similar threats in early July, but the report failed to discuss the circumstances leading to the threats. The report did state that the government responded swiftly to the incidents, with President Salinas calling Castañeda to assure him of a thorough investigation.

Insofar as the incident relates to Castañeda, the State Department's account in the 1990 report contrasted with the testimony of Rona Weitz of Amnesty International before a House subcommittee. Weitz testified that following publication of an article implicating Mexican antinarcotics police in human rights abuses, Castañeda was accused by the Mexican government of making false claims. His secretary was subsequently intercepted on a Mexico City street, threatened with a pistol and questioned regarding the whereabouts of Castañeda's wife and children. Three other men then joined in intimidating her and told her to warn Castañeda he would be killed if he continued with the investigation. Although President Salinas personally telephoned Castañeda (as reported under different circumstances by the State Department) to assure him that the government was not responsible for the incident and to acknowledge his right to freedom of expression, Castañeda's secretary was stopped subsequently and again threatened with death. She eventually identified officers of the PJF as those responsible for the threats.

In 1991, the most sensational case the State Department reported involved the death of physician and columnist Victor Manuel Oropeza, which, according to the report, was the most controversial human rights case during the year. The murder sparked outrage among those who believed he was killed because he had recently written articles critical of the PJF. In the ensuing investigation, María Teresa Jardi, a respected advocate for human rights, and others were critical of the police investigation. Ms. Jardi reportedly left the attorney general's office in protest shortly thereafter. Although arrests were made in the case, the State Department reported that strong doubts remained as to whether those arrested were guilty. These concerns were confirmed by the 1992 report, in which the State Department stated that those arrested had been released and charges were instead brought against several police officers accused of fabricating a case against them.

"Violence and threats against journalists continued to be a serious problem," the State Department wrote in its report for 1992. The report stated that unidentified persons had vandalized the offices of a newspaper publisher in the Yucatán. The same individual received a package bomb shortly after calling for an investigation into the violent eviction by police of protesters from the main town square.

The reports, in general, have not communicated the full gravity of the situation. For example, while reports have frequently cited the work of non-governmental human rights organizations, the 1991 report did not mention that Article 19 cited Mexico as second only to Colombia in numbers of murdered journalists in the Americas that year. Nor did the numbers of incidents reported by the State Department correspond to the findings of Freedom House in its 1991-1992 report, *Freedom in the World,* that "over 20 journalists have been killed or disappeared in the last four years." Also, as noted, the reports have failed to give careful follow-up of cases cited in preceding years and have not provided background data or motives in many of the reported instances, in contrast to cases covered under other sections of the report involving "Political and Other Extrajudicial Killing and Torture and Other Cruel, Inhuman or Degrading Treatment or Punishment."

On September 12, 1990, the Subcommittee on Human Rights and International Organizations and the Subcommittee on Western Hemisphere Affairs of the House Committee on Foreign Affairs held joint hearings on human rights in Mexico. At the hearings, Doug Bereuter (D-NE) noted a report by Americas Watch stating that 51 journalists had been killed in Mexico in the last 18 years. He reacted, "If we are going to understand what is happening in Mexico, I think it is essential that we have an aggressive, strong Mexican press news media."[7]

Ellen Lutz, California Director of Human Rights Watch, testified ". . . Most human rights abuses in Mexico are hidden from public view. This is in part a result of the government's close control over the news media. Press censorship and intimidation of journalists is a recurring theme in Mexico, and most major newspapers are owned by the government or by private individuals with close ties to the government or the PRI. As a result, many human rights stories are never publicized. Follow-up stories about incidents that are reported are even rarer."[8]

Human Rights Monitoring by Mexican Authorities

The 1991 report detailed the activities of the National Human Rights Commission (Comisión Nacional de Derechos Humanos — CNDH — created by the Salinas administration in 1990) related to human rights violations against journalists. It reported that in response to a complaint by the Union of Democratic Journalists, the CNDH began an inquiry in 1990 into 55 cases of alleged denials of human rights to journalists. Of these, according to the 1992 State Department report (which reflected subsequent updates to the CNDH's findings), 40 were concluded, and police investigations pursuant to Commission recommendations continued in the remaining 15. Of the 40 concluded cases, 12 were dropped from the study because they did not involve journalists or after a finding that the incident involved a private dispute. Murderers were convicted in 10 cases, trials were pending against private suspects in three cases (including the murder of Manuel Buendía), and suspects had been identified in two others. Five more cases were dismissed after findings of not guilty, two private citizens accused of murder were acquitted for acting in self-defense, six cases were archived for lack of evidence, and one police officer was convicted of battery. According to the State Department report, in none of the cases did the CNDH establish evidence of a political motive. One of the cases, that of Héctor Félix "El Gato" Miranda, was closed after two men (not public servants) were convicted of murdering him and sentenced to terms of 25 and 27 years. Later, the case was reopened to consider new evidence that others were involved. In addition, six killers involved in the 1988 murder of PAN journalist Linda Bejarano were sentenced to 25- to 27-year terms.

In 1992, the State Department reported that the first stage of the CNDH study of attacks on journalists had been concluded and that the CNDH had announced that it was embarking on the second stage of its study and would investigate 22 new cases.

While the 1991 and 1992 reports cataloged the results of the CNDH investigation extensively, they failed to report the disappointment of some human rights groups that the perpetrators of only three cases actually went to jail. The 1991 report also did not mention that the CNDH itself admitted that state governments often attempted to block the study and that even in cases where persons were imprisoned, the intellectual authors or others responsible for the violence remained unidentified.[9]

Censorship and Access

Since 1977, the reports have reflected an increased tolerance of criticism on the part of the government. Prior to 1986, the reports noted that the press traditionally avoided direct criticism of the president. However, especially since the Salinas administration, these prohibitions appear to have loosened. The 1991 report stated, "Opposition leaders freely voice their criticism of the government, and there are a large number of newspapers and magazines with a wide range of editorial views."

Nonetheless, the reports emphasize that the government has long exercised more subtle control through a monopoly on newsprint, its ability to direct government advertising and the use of "under-the-table" payments to reporters to supplement low wages. In addition, several of the reports have noted that opposition political parties have often charged Mexico's two principal television networks, one [at the time] government-owned and the other privately owned but allegedly partial to the government, with devoting inordinate news coverage to the PRI, particularly at election time.

Article 52 of the federal electoral code provides opposition parties with 15 minutes per month of television time and additional time during an electoral campaign. However, according to the reports, the opposition has asserted that the PRI's advantage derives from its status as Mexico's "official" party and that PRI activities (including campaign events) are covered as if they constitute national news.

The 1990 report notes that one of the more significant steps the government has taken to liberalize the press took place that year, when the government decided to sell off its controlling interest in the state-owned newsprint company, PIPSA. Newspapers and magazines theoretically became free to import newsprint from abroad. However, in order to make PIPSA's sale more attractive to potential buyers, the government moved in June to modify its General Agreement on Tariffs and Trade (GATT) schedule of concessions on four categories of newsprint; modifications included withdrawal of duty-free bindings and increased tariffs (of up to 20 percent) on newsprint imports. According to the State Department report, these modifications effectively limit the competitiveness of foreign suppliers, leaving PIPSA as the main supplier of the country's newsprint.

According to the 1992 report, the government took action that year to decrease the indirect control it exerts over the press when it announced that it would no longer cover expenses incurred by reporters accompanying the president on his travels abroad. In addition, the report stated that at least one newspaper had revised its wage and advertising revenue distribution policies to reduce or eliminate traditional abuses caused by under-the-table payments from public entities to the reporters who cover their activities.

As with its coverage of violence against journalists, the State Department could be more detailed in its reports of coercion and indirect controls on the press. For example, according to Freedom House, newspapers and magazines normally derive over half of all advertising revenues from official sources. Although the reports mention the problem, the State Department made no effort to quantify the effect, and the particular sentence is merely repeated verbatim year after year, suggesting there has been no new research. Moreover, Americas Watch reported that in March 1989, the government coerced Manuel Becerra Acosta, director general of the formerly independent national daily *unomásuno*, to sell the paper, apparently because President Salinas was angry with Becerra for being the first to publicize the existence of the Corriente Democrática, the left opposition movement within the PRI that ultimately split, along with Cuauhtémoc Cárdenas, to form the Democratic Revolutionary Party (Partido de la Revolución Democrática — PRD). Reportedly, the government selectively pressured *unomásuno* to pay its bills and back taxes. Becerra himself was ultimately forced to leave the country. No mention of the incident was made in the State Department reports, even though the matter was fully covered in the media.

As early as 1980, the State Department recognized that standards of freedom of the press varied dramatically among the different regions of Mexico. The 1980 report noted:

> The local press in Baja California Norte and the Yucatán freely attack state government officials, while that in Jalisco appears to exercise greater restraint. When the ex-mayor of Zapopán, Jalisco, was removed from office on charges of corruption and later found dead under questionable circumstances, the local press provided only minimal coverage.[10]

This theme was picked up again in the 1983 report, which noted that "local press freedoms are difficult to gauge since experiences vary from state to state, but there appear to be few institutionalized safeguards against infringement by local authorities."[11]

Conclusion

Human rights matter in U.S. foreign and trade policy. This principle has been directly embodied in U.S. law since as early as 1890, when the McKinley Tariff Act of 1890 forbade the import of goods manufactured with convict labor. Since that time, whatever the defects in implementation, protection of certain fundamental human rights has been embodied both implicitly and explicitly in a wide variety of legislative and policy initiatives. The U.S. government currently collects information on human rights practices in foreign countries through means as diverse as public hearings on practices that violate the workers' rights requirements of the General System of Preferences program to the enormous information-gathering effort involved in the production of the State Department reports.

This information is collected for the express purpose of providing the relevant organs of government with the information they require to take the status of internationally recognized human rights into consideration in the granting of foreign aid or of benefits under certain trade agreements. The information-gathering itself demonstrates the importance of human rights in U.S. foreign and trade policy.

The North American Free Trade Agreement (NAFTA) renders an analysis of the status of freedom of the press in Mexico even more relevant. If for no other reason, a free press insures that there is free and open access to all information, including the status of enforcement of environmental and labor standards intrinsic to the Agreement.

Notes

1. Mexico is a party to numerous international conventions on human rights, including the International Covenant of Civil and Political Rights (1966), the International Covenant on Economic, Social and Cultural Rights (1966), and the American Convention on Human Rights (1969).

Article 19 of the International Covenant of Civil and Political Rights provides:

1. Everyone shall have the right to hold opinions without interference.

2. Everyone shall have the right to freedom of expression; this right shall include freedom to seek, receive and impart information and ideas of all kinds, regardless of frontiers, either orally, in writing or in print, in the form of art, or through any other media of his choice.

3. The exercise of the rights provided for in paragraph 2 of this article carries with it special duties and responsibilities. It may therefore be subject to certain restrictions, but these shall only be such as are provided by law and are necessary:

a. For respect of the rights or reputations of others;

b. For the protection of national security or of public order (*ordre public*), or of public health or morals.

Article 13 of the American Convention on Human Rights provides:

1. Everyone shall have the right to freedom of thought or expression. This right shall include freedom to seek, receive, and impart information and ideas of all kinds, regardless of frontiers, either orally, in writing, in print, in the form of art, or through any other medium of one's choice.

2. The exercise of the right provided for in the foregoing paragraph shall not be subject to prior censorship but shall be subject to subsequent imposition of liability, which shall be expressly established by law to the extent necessary in order to ensure:

a. Respect for the rights or reputations of others; or

b. The protection of national security, public order, or public health or morals.

3. The right of expression may not be restricted by indirect methods or means, such as the abuse of government or private controls over newsprint, radio broadcasting frequencies, or equipment used in the dissemination of information, or by any other means tending to impede the communication and circulation of ideas and opinions.

4. Notwithstanding the provisions of paragraph 2 above, public entertainments may be subject by law to prior censorship for the sole purpose of regulating access to them for the moral protection of childhood and adolescence.

5. Any propaganda for war and any advocacy of national, racial, or religious hatred that constitute incitements to lawless violence or to any other similar illegal action against any person or group of persons on any grounds including those of race, color, religion, language, or national origin shall be considered as offenses punishable by law.

2. Department of State (DOS) instructions for the drafting of this section provide:

Respect for Civil Liberties, Including:

A. Freedom of Speech and Press

In this section discuss freedom of speech, broadcast media, publications and academic freedom in that order. Does the government affirm or deny these rights? Distinguish theory and policy from practice. Are opposition viewpoints freely discussed? Is criticism of government tolerated? Are political meetings subject to surveillance? Describe ownership and control of the media from government ownership and operation of media in general, describe the degree to which some areas of complaint or criticisms of officials may be tolerated. Be precise in describing "self-censorship." Have there been real penalties for offenders? Does the government use indirect means (e.g., control of newsprint supplies, foreign exchange, advertising, licensing, etc.) to influence or control the media? Discuss censorship of books and other publications. Is academic freedom respected? As in other sections, describe any efforts of opposition or terrorist groups to attack or inhibit press, politicians, or other from freely expressing opinions or conducting legitimate activities. Reports on democracies require only brief summary statements that an independent press, an effective judiciary, and a functioning democratic political system combine to ensure freedom of speech and press. If there have been specific instances of abuse in 1991, or significant legal challenges or decisions affecting this area, these should be noted. Reports on countries with mixed records should concentrate on the problem areas. For example, many regimes may allow freedom of speech and press on issues concerning the economy, or foreign affairs, while restricting discussion of domestic politics.

3. Section 116(d)(1) of the Foreign Assistance Act provides:

The Secretary of State shall transmit to the Speaker of the House of Representatives and the Committee on Foreign Relations of the Senate, by January 31 of each year, a full and complete report regarding:

1. the status of internationally recognized human rights, within the meaning of subsection (a) ...

A. in countries that received assistance under this part, and

B. in all other foreign countries which are members of the United Nations and which are not otherwise the subject of a human rights report under this Act.

Section 502(B)(b) of the Foreign Assistance Act provides:

The Secretary of State shall transmit to Congress, as part of the presentation materials for security assistance programs proposed for each fiscal year, a full and complete report, prepared with the assistance of the Assistant Secretary of State for Human Rights and Humanitarian Affairs, with respect to practices regarding the observance of and respect for internationally recognized human rights in each country proposed as a recipient of security assistance.

4. DOS Instructions for the Preparation of the 1991 *Country Reports on Human Rights Practices*, Unclassified Telegram, State 276596 2119062 (1991).

5. Most noteworthy of the 1988 murders was that of TV anchorwoman Linda Bejarano, who was killed in Juárez along with two others when the car she was riding in was sprayed with machine-gun fire. Men who identified themselves as police ordered the car to stop, but Bejarano's husband, who was driving the car, did not stop, believing the men to be robbers.

6. Abuses in connection with various drug enforcement programs have been a long-standing problem in Mexico. Regrettably, the U.S. government has tended to be permissive of these abuses, as was exemplified in congressional hearings in 1990, when Sally G. Cowal, deputy assistant secretary, Bureau for the Caribbean and Mexican Affairs, Department of State, testified: "In the context of our focus today, we should remember that the line between effective law enforcement against violent and well-armed traffickers and the protection of human rights, including those of traffickers, would be a delicate one in any society" (6). This attitude may account for the minimal coverage of this area in the reports.

7. Report of the joint hearings held by the Subcommittee on Human Rights and International Organizations and the Subcommittee on Western Hemisphere Affairs of the House Committee on Foreign Affairs, 30.

8. Report of the joint hearings of the two subcommittees, 81.

9. Lawyers Committee for Human Rights, *Critique: Review of the U.S. Department of State's Country Reports on Human Rights Practices, 1991*, 224. The CNDH is a governmental agency, and its president reports directly to the Mexican president. The CNDH has limited investigatory and no prosecutorial powers and depends upon publicity and the influence of its president to enforce its recommendations. Committee Report, 223.

10. DOS, *Country Reports on Human Rights Practices for 1980* — Mexico.

11. DOS, *Country Reports on Human Rights Practices for 1983* — Mexico.

Chapter 10

The Measure of Violence:
PROBLEMS IN DOCUMENTATION

Joel Solomon

The cases of well-known reporters gunned down in Mexico City and Tijuana have created the impression that journalists in Mexico regularly lose their lives or suffer beatings, threats and kidnappings at the hands of secrecy-crazed government officials or drug traffickers bent on revenge. Analyses of press conditions in Mexico, peppered with statistics showing murder rates for journalists akin to those of Peru and Colombia, often paint a bleak picture of press freedom in Mexico. The sheer number and variety of reported threats, beatings and other offenses — a minimum of 70 or 80 cases reported every year in the Mexico City press alone — are causes for serious concern. In addition, the government's poor record in seeking justice in even the most high-profile of these cases serves to implicate and discredit the authorities. Finding a coherent explanation for the attacks reported in Mexico, however, is far from easy.

The charge that the murder of journalists serves to stifle reporters in Mexico is unsubstantiated. If even a fraction of the reports of nonlethal attacks against journalists were true, such abuses would undoubtedly serve to inhibit some journalists in areas where abuse is common, but much more investigation into all physical attacks is required before an accurate portrayal of their impact on Mexican press freedom can be established. Attacks against journalists in any country can be divided into premeditated attempts to limit freedom of expression or a particular ongoing investigation, the results of

Joel Solomon is research director of Human Rights Watch/Americas. Prior to joining Human Rights Watch, he worked as program director at the Robert F. Kennedy Memorial Center for Human Rights and as associate director and Latin America researcher for the Committee to Protect Journalists.

immediate negative reactions to published stories and abuses completely unrelated to journalism. So much contradictory information exists about these attacks in Mexico that ascertaining into which of these categories a particular attack falls, let alone confirming the basic details of an incident, is difficult. This problem is complicated by the pervasive system of government-sponsored financial incentives for reporters, which has its own effects on reporting independent of attacks on journalists [see Riva Palacio and Keenan, this volume]. Enrique Maza, news editor at the weekly *Proceso*, recognized as the country's leading investigative magazine, asserts, "It's very dangerous in Mexico to make generalizations about whether journalists are being attacked because of their work or not. We can talk about it, but there is insufficient information on which to base conclusions."

Claims that journalists are regularly assassinated in retaliation for their work are not only unproven, they also detract from efforts that deserve more attention, such as pushing the government to account for the murders that have taken place and ensuring that nonlethal physical attacks are halted. Efforts aimed at denouncing physical attacks would be greatly complemented by programs designed to promote reliable documentation on the subject, education about journalists' rights and government accountability for the investigation and prosecution of crimes against journalists.

There are, of course, cases in which government officials have been directly responsible for murders, most notably the 1984 assassination of Manuel Buendía in Mexico City. A prominent journalist with the daily *Excélsior*, Buendía earned his reputation as a hard-hitting investigative reporter unafraid to cover controversial topics. This is one of the clearest press freedom-related assassinations of the five or six dozen journalists' deaths reported in Mexico over the last two decades. Documentation on the case reads like a farce, complete with years of government cover-up and bungling. Eventually, the very officials charged with investigating the murder were implicated. Lucy Conger details the Buendía case elsewhere in this volume and discusses other noted political attacks on journalists, including the 1989 shotgun murder of Héctor Félix Miranda from Tijuana's *Zeta*.

At issue, then, is not whether or not there are documented cases of journalists who have been targeted for their work. Clearly, there are. Neither is the government's will to protect journalists in question, since it has shown little intention of doing so. Rather, the problem has to do with the documentation and interpretation of attacks against journalists in Mexico.

Evaluating Reported Attacks Against Journalists

Reports of the number of journalists murdered in Mexico vary, but recent Mexican and international sources put the figure as high as 61 "killed under suspicious circumstances" between 1982 and the beginning of 1993.[1]

José Alvarez Icaza, who directs the Mexico City-based National Center for Social Communication (Centro Nacional de Comunicación Social — CENCOS), believes there has been a steady increase in the number of journalists killed over the years. "During the Echeverría administration, an average of one journalist was killed every year. During the López Portillo government, two were killed on average each year. During de la Madrid's tenure, the figure jumped to four per year. During the Salinas administration from 1988 through 1992, an average of eight have died every year."

Though many journalists may have come to a violent end in Mexico during those years, in only a handful of these cases can the killing be linked definitively to the journalistic work of the victim. Analyses focusing on the overall number of deaths, even when they provide brief caveats about the unclear nature of the information, tend to lead to the inevitable conclusion that murdering journalists is a habitual recourse for those in Mexico who wish to keep information out of public view.

In fact, the link between journalism and the murders is far too tenuous to lead to such a conclusion. "Say there were 100 journalists killed in the last 10 years," says Jesús Blancornelas, editor of the Tijuana publication *Zeta*, which counts the case of its slain columnist Héctor Félix among the clear political assassinations of journalists documented in Mexico. "I'd say nine or 10 may have been killed for their work as journalists." Teresa Gil, a member of the Journalists' Defense Commission of the Union of Democratic Journalists (Unión de Periodistas Democráticos — UPD), which submitted for investigation a list of murdered journalists to the government's Human Rights Commission in 1990, named a handful of murder cases in which the murders were clearly linked to the work of the journalists killed. About one of every reported 10 cases was clear.

The information needed to make accurate determinations about motives is lacking. A combination of inaccurate, partisan reporting and poor follow-up in the press makes it difficult to rely on news reporting to learn details of cases. Critics of the Mexican press point out that journalists often respond to their bosses' or their own economic interests rather than the interests of news dissemination. In *Revista de Comunicación Mexicana*, Raymundo Riva Palacio has highlighted the role of corruption, rather than fear, in keeping Mexican journalists quiet. "Generally in Mexico, journalists cross with great ease the line that divides them from power, openly letting themselves be seduced," he argues. "To talk about eradicating self-censorship is really to talk about democratization in the news media and of political society as a whole."

For these reasons, the Committee's standard methodology has proved inadequate in Mexico. In most countries, press reports can be verified independently by contacting colleagues of the journalists involved in the incidents, human rights organizations and others with firsthand knowledge of the situation. To act on a case, the Committee to Protect Journalists needs, at a minimum, to be able to confirm the date an incident took place, the names and professional affiliations of the journalists involved and the circumstances under which the attack occurred. In many places in Latin America, it is sometimes necessary to make multiple calls to such people in order to iron out details, but it is far more common in Mexico to receive contradictory information from press and firsthand sources than in any other country in the hemisphere. Excellent human rights and press freedom organizations within Mexico do not have the capability to verify all reported attacks independently. Making more calls to Mexico from abroad does not always lead to more clarity.

Early in 1993, for example, a human rights organization in Reynosa, Tamaulipas, informed the Committee of several attacks against journalists in the area in 1992, some involving the daily newspaper *El Gráfico*. The managing editor confirmed details of some of the incidents to the Committee but denied major elements of other reported cases involving his newspaper. Confirming the dates and details of other attacks in Tamaulipas was difficult. Even when talking directly to those who suffered attacks, dates conflicted, and details about the reported incidents were vague.

There may be several explanations for the Tamaulipas example: the editor at the newspaper involved may not have been informed of the attacks in question; the editor's interests may have been best served by withholding certain data; the editor may not have cared about the attacks suffered by other reporters at the paper; the human rights organization may have received some misinformation. The Committee to Protect Journalists lacked the resources to send a researcher to Tamaulipas to interview enough people to make an accurate determination about the cases.

The Tamaulipas situation was not unique. In 1992, a press freedom organization reported that the Mexico City daily *unomásuno* had been raided by a former government official on June 11 and that journalists at the newspaper had been threatened. When contacted by telephone by the Committee to Protect Journalists, however, an editor at the newspaper could not recall any such raid. When the incident was explained as reported, he remembered and commented, "Oh, that. That was a lovers' problem." The would-be attacker, he said, had entered the newsroom looking for a journalist. When a colleague intervened to assist the journalist, he was threatened.

The Committee did not report the incident, not because it valued the latter report more than the initial one, but because there was a credible alternative explanation by the news medium involved. *Unomásuno*, a major daily, was easy to contact. Often in Mexico, newspapers outside Mexico City are more difficult to contact, and reaching a reliable source at the paper is an even greater challenge.

There are cases in which sufficient information exists to lay to rest rumors of links between attacks and journalism, but even in those cases, news of the attack sometimes gets swept up into the flow of press-freedom information. Mario Elias Medina Valenzuela, for example, was shot to death on June 28, 1990, in a restaurant in the city of Durango. "Mexican Journalist Gunned Down by Unknown Assailants," Reuters reported the next day. The story listed several of Medina's previous journalistic affiliations, then pegged the report to another well-known case, as if to suggest a press-related motive to the Medina assassination. "Medina's murder came as former senior police officers were being questioned in connection with the April 1984 killing of leading Mexican journalist Manuel Buendía," it said.

An adamant editor at *El Sol de Durango*, where Medina had worked 12 years earlier, informed the Committee the next day that the murder was unrelated to journalism and that Medina hadn't even worked as a journalist for years. "Everyone knows that the Medinas have a long-standing feud with the Rentería family," the editor said. The National Human Rights Commission later found Atanacio and Manuel Aldaco Rentería guilty of the murder, listing the case as "without any relationship to journalism."

Analysis of Reported Attacks Against Journalists

The fact that some cases are unclear does not necessarily mean the attacks in question had nothing to do with the journalists' work or that they should be ignored. CENCOS's Alvarez Icaza suggests that murders in Mexico are murky because government officials there are more subtle than their South American counterparts at creating unclear circumstances surrounding the deaths of reporters. But even without ascribing the lack of clarity in Mexico or anywhere to conspiracy, unclear cases should often be included in analyses of attacks on journalists. Including them may lead to a more complete understanding of the conditions in which journalists work. However, given the difficulty in documenting attacks in Mexico and the frequency with which contradictory information surfaces there, basing analyses on reported attacks without further investigation is highly problematic.

In an attempt to clarify accusations about the government's involvement in attacks against journalists, the Mexican magazine *Revista de Comunicación Mexicana*, published by the Manuel Buendía Foundation, conducted a broad survey of newspaper reports of such attacks, combing eight major newspapers in Mexico City for information. Between January 1989 and January 1992, the magazine searched some 7,000 newspaper editings and found 209 reported attacks. A later search for 1992 netted some 80 incidents, indicating about the same yearly rate of attack.

Because it is based only on Mexican press reports, the study would need extensive independent confirmation before its findings could be used to draw final conclusions, but it provides an important insight into the kind of information about the news media that circulates in Mexico. Of the 24 journalists and four non-journalist media workers killed between 1989 and 1991 — more than nine per year, on average — only 12 percent of the murders were identified as press related — an average of one every year of the study. Drug traffickers were not listed as a force against journalists in the study. The study found that 33 percent of the attacks were committed by the "forces of order," 10 percent by government officials and 18 percent by "institutions of the government"; however, without knowing which of the attacks with press freedom-related motives were committed by these state employees, it is impossible to measure the government's role in limiting press freedom.

By far the greatest single problem faced by journalists, according to the 1989-1991 study, is nonlethal physical attacks (44 percent of all incidents), followed by threats and assassinations (13 percent and 14 percent, respectively). The study asserted that a journalist was attacked in Mexico every five days but found that less than half of the attacks (48 percent) had to do with the journalists' work. Nonetheless, the only potential interpretation the magazine offered was that "the temptation to silence or control the media is latent in the public and private arenas...." The study seemed to confirm that newspaper articles decrying attacks against journalists cannot always be used to analyze press freedom and that, in the case of Mexico, one must proceed with caution.

One interpretation of the study places less emphasis on the conspiracy of officials to limit press freedom through violence and gives more attention to the system that has engendered the financial corruption of the media. Physical attacks may be the result of officials acting in retaliation when financial incentives fail to maintain silence. "It's like the relationship between the master and the slave when the slave rebels," says Enrique Maza of *Proceso*. Authorities expect compliance and are angered when the press does not automatically follow the lead of the government. Such attacks are as unacceptable as any other, but they might have less overall impact on press freedom than the kind of systemic attempts to limit the press that have plagued Guatemala's journalists for years. Journalists may be targeted for murder, but no pattern emerges from their deaths.

Even those who question the pervasiveness of physical attacks or the impact of abuses on press freedom do not doubt that real press freedom-related attacks take place and that certain regions in Mexico are more dangerous than others. Also, whether or not an attack is aimed at silencing a particular journalist, it can have a detrimental impact on press freedom. Even in cases where the motives behind the attacks are unclear, abuses chill freedom of expression by creating uncertainty about what will and will not be accepted by those who attack journalists.

Toward Systematic Accounting of Attacks

It should not be concluded that journalists are safe in Mexico. Clearly, they are not. Perhaps different approaches to documentation and denunciation of attacks against journalists have more to do with differences in tactics than they do with long-term goals. The UPD, for example, will continue to denounce all murder cases, even if they are unclear in nature. "As long as the assassinations of journalists are not clarified, we blame the government," says Teresa Gil. "We've seen so much government omission and cover-up." She says the problem is that the government has not fulfilled its obligation to investigate attacks and prosecute those who commit them.

The UPD has made the appropriate representations to the government to seek investigations of cases, but others question the efficacy of such moves. *Proceso's* Enrique Maza, for example, suggests that pushing cases without more independent investigation allows the government to wash its hands of the issue. Others question whether focusing on physical attacks without considering the context of the broader system of press controls makes sense. However, despite these differences, there are concrete steps that can be taken to provide physical safety for journalists in Mexico.

Several international press freedom organizations conferred in 1992 to develop strategies for overcoming the problem of differences in the groups' murder statistics from around the world. The organizations determined that greater discussion of each case was essential, so that conclusions could be drawn from the best available information. In Mexico, such a step is necessary, but a further step is also needed. Mechanisms should be established for overcoming the problems in documentation. Domestic and international human rights organizations have expanded their work in Mexico in recent years and could add a component designed to focus on journalists' rights. Such a program might include a detailed analysis of the state of documentation of attacks against journalists in Mexico and proposals for overcoming the problems. It might educate journalists about their rights in order to establish a common basis for consideration of the problems Mexican journalists face.

The goal should be to document, with as much detail as possible, every attack against a journalist, no matter how seemingly unimportant, and to do so in a clearly nonpartisan way. In El Salvador, starting in the mid-1980s, such documentation helped force the government of El Salvador and its international supporters to recognize and work to correct the systemic abuses committed against journalists. Confronted with enough detail to establish clear patterns, the government of El Salvador had to end its abuses of the press. It may be, as *Zeta's* Jesús Blancornelas suggests, that the economic interests of corrupt journalists will render such programs meaningless, but the fact that journalists have organized to protect themselves against abuses in Mexico indicates that a demand for this type of work exists.

Mexico's size may work against journalists trying to organize nationally, but it is not an insurmountable obstacle. Just recently in Peru, journalists from throughout the country who were interested in documenting attacks and working to prevent new ones formed a group. Establishing a flow of information independent of the entrenched, politicized groups that already exist there will be key to their work. International organizations interested in stemming the abuse of journalists in Mexico should assist their local colleagues in establishing efficient networks and obtaining funding sufficient to meet their goals.

Tentative Conclusions

It is tempting to connect physical attacks against journalists with Mexican government policy, either as a first or last resort for silencing reporters. But there is inconclusive evidence for that connection. Likewise, the role of physical attacks in limiting press freedom in Mexico is not clear. Murders may send shock waves through journalists' circles, says *Proceso*'s Maza, but they don't work as a general tool to silence the press. While he admits that the purpose of the murder might be to scare off others in the media, he says, "It's like the death penalty. They say it is a warning to others, but it's so extreme that it can't become common." Certainly, it is not government policy to investigate such cases, but until more information exists about the nature of physical attacks against journalists throughout Mexico, pronouncements about the impact of physical attacks on press freedom can only be tentative.

If the government of Mexico is culpable of anything, it is for failing to investigate fully cases that have been documented. By maintaining silence, the government has created an atmosphere in which it seems acceptable for journalists to be beaten up. The task for journalists and international journalists' rights monitors in Mexico is to establish viable mechanisms that can detail the motives and intricacies of attacks against journalists.

One thing that is clear about the press in Mexico is the unique, systemic nature of the forces that affect journalists. *Zeta* editor Blancornelas, perhaps cynical after years of pushing those forces to provide justice in the case of his slain colleague Héctor Félix, suggests everyone is to blame. "Freedom of expression exists," he says. "It's just not used."

Note

1. "Presentation by PEN Canada and The Canadian Committee to Protect Journalists to the Provincial Cabinet Committee on NAFTA," April 8, 1993, Toronto, Canada. The London-based Article 19 said in 1989 that at least 51 were killed between 1970 and 1988, while the Mexican daily *Excélsior* reported in 1990 that 40 had been assassinated between 1982 and 1990.

Epilogue

Chapter 11

Limits to Apertura:
PROSPECTS FOR PRESS FREEDOM IN THE NEW FREE-MARKET MEXICO

Jorge G. Castañeda

U ntil the Mexican government decides — or is forced to decide — that a relatively free media, despite its risks, is preferable to the authoritarian status quo, there is no hope for change. And nothing that happened under President Carlos Salinas de Gortari suggested that he made such a decision. In a much more sophisticated fashion than critics thought possible and in a much more effective manner than apologists for the political system imagined, the Salinas government retained control over the media.

President Salinas actually had less political incentive to liberalize the media than previous administrations. Salinas' predecessors loathed the idea of a free and vigorous press, but the absence of an opposition, the prevalence of economic growth and the adequate functioning of the political system made direct censorship and control largely dispensable. However, after 1988, that was no longer the case. To overcome the trauma of the 1988 elections, the lack of economic growth for nearly a decade and the increasingly rusted and worn gears of the old authoritarian machinery, control of information and expectations assumed a new importance.

Jorge G. Castañeda, a regular columnist for the Los Angeles Times, Newsweek *'s Latin American edition and other publications, is professor of political science at Mexico's National Autonomous University. His most recent book among the eight he has authored or co-authored,* The Mexican Stock, *was published by The New Press in 1995. He is currently writing a biography of Che Guevara, which will be published in 1997 by Knopf.*

Whether in the context of the real terms of the 1989 debt renegotiation, the true political prospects for the North American Free Trade Agreement's (NAFTA) passage in the United States, the terms and benefits of the privatization of state-run enterprises or, finally, the true state of the economy, it became almost indispensable for the government to micromanage information. As a result of the government's need to continue electoral tampering (without the embarrassing revelations and sloppiness of 1988), keeping the media away from polls, recounts and observers also acquired a new relevance. This meant doling out information slowly — even the final, detailed results of the 1991 elections were only released to the public in late 1993 — and guaranteeing that the media not complain too much. It also implied making sure that few media outlets would attempt to generate their own electoral information: quick counts, exit polls, pre-election polls and detailed monitoring of electoral rolls and spending remain scant or nonexistent. Indeed, because of the enormous role expectations have played in the Salinas economic strategy, and in view of the critical need to recreate the impression of the Institutional Revolutionary Party's (Partido Revolucionario Institucional — PRI) invincibility, control over the media has become more important than ever. Unprecedented levels of corruption have been added to unprecedented sensitivity to coverage of that corruption; thus, a stronger grip on the media has been a logical characteristic of the Salinas administration. It is worth dwelling on the characteristics of this control; in the Mexican media, as in other endeavors, the devil is in the details.

A good case in point was the Salinas administration's sale of two state-owned television channels. Together with the privatization of the state newsprint monopoly, PIPSA, announced with much fanfare by President Salinas at the 1989 meeting of the Inter American Press Association (IAPA) in Monterrey, the sale of the two TV channels was meant to be the centerpiece of media reform in Mexico. The government finally announced the results of the bidding at the end of July 1993. But the sale of the television network turned out to be a dramatic nonevent, like the still-unconsummated PIPSA sale. (The newsprint enterprise is still in state hands, even though it no longer has a monopoly on the selling or importing of newsprint.)

The channels were sold to an appliance chain store owner, Ricardo Benjamín Salinas Pliego [no relation to the president], for $645 million. The second-place bid was 30 percent less than the winning bid, but by the time final bids were received, many potential purchasers had pulled out. Foreign television interests had already withdrawn, concluding that the price was too high and the caps on foreign equity ownership were too restrictive. Mexico's Multivisión (owned by Joaquín Vargas) also canceled its bid, reportedly after being tipped off that the nod had already been given to Salinas Pliego. Televisa was never allowed to participate, since ostensibly the purpose of the entire exercise was to begin to break Emilio Azcárraga's iron grip on Mexican television. But many analysts concluded that the final sale had accomplished just the opposite: by declaring Salinas Pliego the winner, the government had strengthened Televisa by ensuring that it would have no serious competition. The decision in favor of the appliance-store magnate was a telltale sign of the government's true intentions — to keep Televisa powerful, the new company weak and in debt and to restrict mass media ownership to Mexican-style "politically correct" captains of industry.

Their conclusions were well-founded. First, the Salinas Pliego group had no media experience whatsoever, other than selling televisions in its bargain-basement department stores. Second, the amount of money paid — well above the second-place bid and far above any reasonable assessment of the true value acquired — in conjunction with the limited resources of Elektra, Salinas Pliego's company, practically guaranteed that the new owners would spend little money on programming, renovation or other investment in the network. Finally, the political and social opinions voiced by Salinas Pliego soon after being awarded the channels ("I didn't buy these channels to criticize the government. Besides, Mexico is not ready for democracy. Television is mainly for entertainment and for women, who belong at home.") also insured that Televisa's hold on news programming would not be questioned by the new company. Salinas Pliego, like Azcárraga, openly proclaimed his support for and admiration of President Salinas and the PRI regime. It came as no surprise that soon after his successful bid, Salinas Pliego announced that he might sell the movie theaters he had acquired in the privatization package to Televisa. He also met with Azcárraga, requesting that Televisa sell programming to the new company, Televisión Azteca.

If the Mexican government had intended the privatization of its television network to weaken Televisa or create any form of competition, a number of easier and much more effective options were available. The first, of course, was simply divestiture (the AT&T solution). Any one of a number of antimonopoly, public service or other laws on the books — or simply sheer pressure — could have been applied to Televisa. Azcárraga's network owns four channels in Mexico City, a large number of local stations, a radio network, the country's largest cable company and many other ventures. Just by forcing it to divest itself of part of its television holdings — "privatizing Televisa," as some commentators put it — would have broken its monopolistic hold.

Alternatively, the Salinas adminstration could have allowed either of the two U.S. Spanish-language networks to enter Mexico, not only through cable (limited to 100,000 subscribers in a nation of 90 million people) but on the airwaves. Both Univisión and Telemundo expressed interest, had the required resources in association with other ventures and would have represented a serious, perhaps fatal threat to Televisa. Instead of encouraging and permitting this as an alternative to forced divestiture, the authorities supported Azcárraga's preemptive strike: with two partners whose real interests in the matter were dubious, Azcárraga acquired a major equity stake in Univisión, eliminating it as a source of potential competition. Meanwhile, Telemundo took the hint that foreign Spanish-language television was not welcomed by the Mexican authorities and has never truly sought to establish itself in Mexico other than as a feed for a non-Televisa cable network. Finally, the authorities could have sold off the state-owned network to any of the several viable bidders.

In fact, the incestuous link with Televisa is a mainstay of the PRI regime, just as government protection remains essential to the corporation's enormous profits. Azcárraga's media ventures beyond Mexican borders and the PRI's mantle have failed miserably. His first attempt to set up a full-service Spanish-language television network in the United States foundered in 1986, when the Federal Communications Commission (FCC) ruled that his stake exceeded the legal limits on ownership of U.S. television stations and networks by non-U.S. nationals. His U.S. nationwide sports daily, *The National,* a multimillion-dollar venture, folded after barely a year. Without the government's backing, Televisa would lose its privileged position as the sole mass-audience vehicle for advertisers, actors and singers. Without Televisa's monopoly and its mass audience, the Mexican political system would lose its main instrument of public opinion.

The government exercises control over media outlets in direct proportion to the size of their audience. Large-circulation national newspapers are more closely monitored than low-circulation local papers, and the control the government exercises over print media is nothing compared to its control over broadcast media.

While the local print media is almost totally free of overt federal interference (there have been exceptions, such as when *El Norte* of Monterrey had its newsprint supply cut off briefly in the 1970s and when the recently founded *Siglo 21* of Guadalajara experienced harassment from government licensing bureaus), the national dailies and weeklies are more vulnerable. The greater the circulation, the stronger — though not always more successful — the efforts of the central government to censor what it considers crucial or damaging.

Since the early 1970s and Julio Scherer's *Excélsior,* at least one well-known publication in Mexico City has always been systematically publishing stories and opinions critical of the government: *Excélsior* from 1969 through 1976, *Proceso* from 1976 through today, *unomásuno* from 1977 through 1983, *La Jornada* from 1983 to the present and *El Financiero* in recent times. While always subject to pressure and financial constraints, these publications have remained relatively open and critical of the government, although as we shall see shortly, there are significant differences within each publication as to what can and cannot be published.

Barnes & Noble Bookseller
4950 Pacific   Space 319

472-1885

11-24   920 R011

Larousse Conc   Spanish   11.95
2035420172

SUB TOTAL   11.95
SALES TAX   .93
TOTAL   12.88
AMOUNT TENDERED
CASH   20.00

TOTAL PAYMENT   20.00
CHANGE   7.12

Thank you for shopping at
Barnes & Noble Booksellers

Booksellers since 1873

days with a receipt from any Barnes & Noble store.
Store Credit issued for new and unread books and unopened music after 30
days or without a sales receipt. Credit issued at <u>lowest sale price</u>.
We gladly accept returns of new and unread books and unopened music from
bn.com with a bn.com receipt for store credit at the bn.com price.

Full refund issued for new and unread books and unopened music within 30
days with a receipt from any Barnes & Noble store.
Store Credit issued for new and unread books and unopened music after 30
days or without a sales receipt. Credit issued at <u>lowest sale price</u>.
We gladly accept returns of new and unread books and unopened music from
bn.com with a bn.com receipt for store credit at the bn.com price.

Full refund issued for new and unread books and unopened music within 30
days with a receipt from any Barnes & Noble store.
Store Credit issued for new and unread books and unopened music after 30
days or without a sales receipt. Credit issued at <u>lowest sale price</u>.
We gladly accept returns of new and unread books and unopened music from
bn.com with a bn.com receipt for store credit at the bn.com price.

Full refund issued for new and unread books and unopened music within 30
days with a receipt from any Barnes & Noble store.

The behind-the-scenes maneuvering that took place in the so-called Cordobagate affair in November 1992 provided a case study of the government's ranking of the print media. Soon after the U.S. election, President Salinas' chief aide and virtual alter ego, José Córdoba, traveled to Washington to meet with the Clinton transition team and obtain assurances that the new administration would go forward with NAFTA. The Washington correspondents for *Proceso* and *El Financiero* discovered the time and venue of Córdoba's meeting with Samuel Berger and Barry Carter, Clinton's representatives. They occupied a table adjoining Berger and Carter's at the Montpelier Restaurant in the Madison Hotel. They overheard much of the conversation without being noticed, since Córdoba, despite the immense power he wields, remains largely unfamiliar with the cast of characters in the Mexican media. *El Financiero* ran a two-part summary of the conversation (an embarrassing exchange for Córdoba, since he seemed to be pleading with Berger and receiving only scant guarantees in return) on Thursday and Friday, November 25 and 26. *Proceso* was preparing a cover story on the conversation for that Sunday, when on Friday evening, Minister of Internal Affairs Fernando Gutiérrez Barrios dropped in to see Julio Scherer, the publisher of the weekly, to ask him, on behalf of the president and on grounds of national security, not to run the story. Scherer countered by reminding Gutiérrez Barrios that he was being asked to spike a story that had already been published. The minister's answer was categorical: *El Financiero*, with a circulation of less than 50,000, predominantly in Mexico City, was one thing; *Proceso*, with its circulation of over 100,000 throughout the country and in all sectors of society, was another. (Scherer's answer was just as categorical: he ran the story.)

With a few significant exceptions, however, Mexican government interference with the print media is neither systematic nor heavy-handed. Radio is a different matter, though again there are classes and degrees. Commercial radio expanded considerably during the final years of the de la Madrid administration and the first two years of the Salinas presidency, mainly through the boldness and enormous audience attained by the four-hour morning news show of José Gutiérrez Vivo and Radio Red (owned by Clemente Serna, a member of an unsuccessful investor group in the bid for Channels 7 and 13). Government authorities monitor the program minute by minute. When criticism becomes too strong, either the Ministry of Internal Affairs or the presidential spokesman's office asks — or insists — that Gutiérrez Vivo refrain from discussing certain subjects, inviting certain commentators or further investigating certain allegations. The smaller the station's audience, the less control there is: Radio Universidad and Radio Educación traditionally have been relatively free of government interference, but their audience is limited to intellectuals and a few students. Similarly, local radio stations in the provinces — even in larger cities such as Monterrey and Guadalajara — are less restrained than their counterparts in the capital.

Television is the main focus of the government's efforts at audience control. The numbers tell the story: on a good day, *La Jornada* or *El Financiero* sells approximately 50,000 copies (the former, a bit more; the latter, a few less); the paid circulation of *Excélsior*, the largest and perhaps the only national newspaper in Mexico, does not reach 100,000. A notably newsworthy week will enable *Proceso* to boost sales to 120,000, which means approximately 500,000 readers will get their news from the magazine, since it has a particularly high readership per issue. But roughly 15 million homes in Mexico have television; the nightly audience for Jacobo Zabludovsky's newscast is close to 20 million viewers. To speak only of the print media in Mexico (as in much of Latin America, where millions received television sets and transmission in their homes before they became functionally literate) is to miss the big picture, so to speak.

Thus, it is no coincidence that the most censored, restricted and uncritical reporting and news gathering take place on television, inside the private virtual monopoly that has ruled Mexican television since its birth — Televisa. The opposition never appears on its nightly news shows (this is also true of the formerly state-owned networks, but they captured such a small share of the audience that their performance was hardly relevant); up to half the time is devoted to presidential activities (José López Portillo and Luis Echeverría were covered as apologetically as Salinas). Unpleasant or danger-ous news items are simply not reported. If they are, it is always in the context of favorable reports that "drown out" the negative; the government's spin is gospel. There are no debate shows on Televisa, no Sunday morning talk shows, no special election coverage, exit polling or polling of any sort. There is only what Emilio Azcárraga, the sole owner of Televisa, calls "entertain-ment" for the Mexican people, who will always be, as he said recently, "un pueblo de jodidos [vulgar term meaning bumbling idiots]." Moreover, since Televisa's domination stems primarily from its privileged relationship with the state, which in turn derives enormous benefits from the status quo, it has no incentive to change.

Thus, the often undetected paradox: when it doesn't really matter, the media are relatively open. When things really matter, the media are totally closed. One of the advantages of this arrangement is that foreign correspon-dents with barely adequate Spanish can read — or have translated — critical editorials in *La Jornada* or damaging investigative reports in *Proceso*. But they cannot follow the nightly newscast's rapid-fire language. As a result, many foreigners have the impression that there is a freewheeling debate taking place in the Mexican media.

This basic distinction between print media and television does not mean, however, that the government is indifferent to what the print journalists say or do. The authorities fully realize that the country's political, intellectual and business elites do not watch Zabludovsky but do read *Proceso* and columns such as those by Miguel Angel Granados Chapa in *Reforma* and Carlos Ramírez in *El Financiero*. Government authorities can be extremely sensitive to criticism from these quarters and, on occasion, heavy-handed when it comes to news items that could damage official credibility or make markets nervous.

This fundamental difference between the print media and television and between the mass media and the low-circulation political and intellectual press corresponds to another distinction — the one between editorial comment and hard news reporting. The Mexican government has only rarely become terribly upset over opinions, even those expressed by the nation's foremost columnists. When Lorenzo Meyer blasts specific government officials on the front page of *Excélsior*, they become quite irritated. But in general, the authorities have tolerated dissenting opinions. There is a long tradition of distinguished editorializing in the Mexican press; over the past quarter-century, figures such as Meyer, Daniel Cosío Villegas, Francisco Martínez de la Vega, Manuel Buendía (somewhat more of a muckraker), Granados Chapa and others have filled the pages of Mexico's dailies and weeklies. When the papers that welcomed them were reined in, bought off or shut down, these columnists quickly relocated to other publications, where the authorities allowed them to continue their criticism.

Hard news, however, is a different story. Opinions, regardless of the stature of those who convey them, can be dismissed, ignored or rebutted; actual information cannot. For example, the authorities did not mind a commentator writing that the May 1993 assassination of Cardinal Posadas in Guadalajara represented a serious blow to law and order and that President Salinas was responsible for this breakdown. But when drug traffickers claimed they had been trying to kill another person with a similar car and authorities apprehended a drug trafficker by the name of Joaquín "El Chapo" Guzmán (presumably the intended victim), the government told editors and publishers in no uncertain terms that it would be wise to stop prying into the case and let the judicial authorities pursue their investigation. For the most part, the media complied.

In Mexico, as anywhere, newspapers become successful and increase circulation and advertising only when they become sources of information — not only of opinions, as interesting and informed as they may be. Most Mexican newspapers remain small and weak, with precarious finances, excessively vulnerable to pressure from any source. The two partial exceptions — *Proceso* and *El Norte* — have been successful mostly because they report hard news, although even their best efforts have been frustrated by difficulties in maintaining essential contacts with government sources and by pressure from advertisers loath to offend the authorities.

The Mexican business sector appears to have concluded that the press is not a wise investment: a profitable press is too risky, and a safe press (one that does not threaten its own relationship with the government) is too unprofitable. The print media have never attracted large investments from the private sector. There have been some newspaper moguls in Mexico (Colonel García Valseca in the past, fictionally portrayed by Carlos Fuentes' *The Death of Artemio Cruz;* former United Press International (UPI) owner Mario Vázquez Raña today), but, by and large, business and the print media have not mixed well. This is partly the result of the government's involvement — why risk profitable business connections or privileges provided by the state by engaging in an activity that entails serious risks of confrontation with that same state?

This was the case with *El Independiente*, the only attempt (until *Reforma,* the Mexico City version of *El Norte,* which debuted on November 20, 1993) to set up a new, national and theoretically independent daily during the Salinas era. Javier Moreno Valle, a young, dynamic businessman with superb family and political connections, set out to found a new paper at the beginning of the Salinas term. He assembled what was arguably the best team of honest journalists ever put together in Mexico, purchased a splendid layout from Europe and spent nearly $1 million in training, planning and initial investment. He thought — wrongly, it turned out — that his entire effort had the blessing of the government and, in particular, of former presidential aspirant and Salinas-team token liberal, Manuel Camacho Solís. But some time before the launch, according to leading Mexican journalists who were intimately involved with the newspaper project, Moreno Valle was apprised of the fact that the authorities did not think his testing of the journalistic waters was a good idea and that if he insisted on pursuing this new venture, his other businesses would suffer. He backed off. Why risk birds in the hand for a newspaper in the bush, particularly when the latter could only succeed with the government's blessing?

None of the new Mexican tycoons — Carlos Slim, Roberto Hernández, Roberto González — has expressed any interest in the press, either as a financier or as an advertiser, although the newly privatized phone company has liberalized its advertising policy somewhat.

As long as Televisa dominates the mass media the way it does, very little can change in Mexican television. And as long as private investment in the print media remains low, little can change in print journalism either.

The opening of the Mexican media remains on the country's agenda: it will either occur on President Zedillo's watch or sometime in the next century. At best, guarded optimism is warranted — after Cuba and perhaps Haiti, Mexico certainly has the least-free press of any country in Latin America.

Appendix:
Mexican Journalistes Murdered in the Line of Duty between 1984 and 1995

The Committee to Protect Journalists

O ver the past decade, the Committee to Protect Journalists (CPJ) has collected evidence and published reports on more than 300 cases of journalists who were murdered as a direct consequence of their professional work as reporters, editors, publishers or broadcasters. Between 1984 and 1995, CPJ documented 10 such cases in Mexico, which are listed below. For many other cases of journalists being killed in Mexico over this period, circumstantial but inconclusive evidence exists of a linkage between their murders and their work. In 11 of those cases, also listed here, CPJ continues to press Mexican authorities for further investigations.

This chronological listing begins with the most notorious and arguably most serious of these cases, the May 1984 murder of Manuel Buendía Tellezgirón, the most widely read Mexican investigative reporter of his generation. In the decade prior to Buendía's death, at least eight other Mexican journalists were murdered in apparent reprisals for their reporting. Because these murders took place before CPJ began investigating such crimes, they were never corroborated independently by CPJ researchers.

All the cases listed below were investigated by CPJ staff researchers. More than one source corroborated key details of each incident, information about the victim and the likelihood of linkage between the murder and the victim's work as a journalist. There are many other reported cases for which no such probable causality could be established. Some appear to have been common crimes without political intent or impact. In other cases, murders of individuals who have worked in Mexico's news media appeared to be linked to political activities, not journalism. While such assassinations constitute serious human rights violations, they cannot be categorized as attacks against members of the press as such.

Because the list below omits cases for which evidence appears inconclusive or contradictory, it undoubtedly understates the severity and scope of the problem. In Mexico, as in many countries where journalists are murdered, such crimes are rarely investigated thoroughly or impartially by local or national law enforcement agencies. Successful prosecutions are the exception to the rule. The CPJ welcomes additional information about these cases and any other murders of journalists who were targeted because of their profession.

1984

Manuel Buendía Tellezgirón, *Excélsior*
Date of Death: May 30, 1984
Place of Death: Mexico City, Mexico

Buendía, a prominent syndicated columnist for the daily *Excélsior*, was shot to death on a street corner near his office in downtown Mexico City by a young gunman who fled. The then-director of the Federal Security Directorate (Directorio Federal de Seguridad — DFS), José Antonio Zorrilla Pérez, a close acquaintance of and source for Buendía, was the first senior national police official at the murder scene; he also assumed control of the investigation. The columnist's colleagues said he had been working on columns about official collusion with drug traffickers. An initial investigation into the murder was marked by the loss of and tampering with evidence and apparent official reluctance to question Buendía's many high-level sources in federal and state police agencies. Five years later, following a change of government, Zorrilla Pérez was charged with ordering Buendía's murder. (In the interim, Zorrilla Pérez resigned as DFS director and became a ruling-party candidate for Congress.) The subsequently reorganized DFS, part of the powerful Ministry of Governance, was itself a powerful and notoriously corrupt national plainclothes police agency engaged in domestic political surveillance and investigation (and, critics say, protection) of drug trafficking. Zorrilla and Juan Rafael Moro Avila, another former DFS officer, were convicted and sentenced to 35 years in prison for the murder. Three former federal police officers were convicted as co-conspirators and sentenced to 25 years in prison.

Javier Juárez Vázquez, *Primera Plana*
Date of Death: May 30, 1984
Place of Death: Coatzalcoalcos, Veracruz

Juárez Vázquez, director of the weekly *Primera Plana* in Coatzalcoalcos, Veracruz, was found shot to death in this port city with his hands tied and his body bearing signs of torture. His colleagues believed he was murdered because of his investigations into ties between drug traffickers and high-ranking federal officials. National press coverage of his murder was obscured by front-page accounts of the same-day murder of the more widely known Manuel Buendía. In 1990, U.S. Drug Enforcement Administration (DEA) sources in Mexico were quoted by local reporters as saying that the 1984 murder was ordered by then-Minister of Governance, Manuel Bartlett Díaz. Bartlett, a candidate for (and subsequently elected) governor of the state of Puebla, vehemently denied the charges.

1986

Ernesto Flores Torrijos, *El Popular*
Date of Death: July 17, 1986
Place of Death: Matamoros, Tamaulipas

Flores Torrijos, editor of *El Popular*, a newspaper in Matamoros, Tamaulipas, was killed by unidentified gunmen as he walked to his office. Also murdered was his colleague, Norma Alicia Moreno Figueroa (see below). At the time, it was widely assumed in the state that Flores Torrijos' murder was linked to his aggressive coverage of drug trafficking and related local police corruption. According to newspaper reports, the *El Popular* office had police protection that was withdrawn two days before the journalist was gunned down. The two alleged assassins, Saúl Hernández Rivera and Jesús Avila Fabián, were killed shortly after by unidentified assailants. The former prosecutor in charge of the case, María del Refugio Martínez Cruz, closed the case after Hernández and Avila were killed. A 1991 report by the federal government's National Human Rights Commission (Comisión Nacional de Derechos Humanos — CNDH) underscored the seeming unwillingness of state authorities to investigate, calling their handling of the case a "clear denial of justice." The Commission report noted the suspicious disappearance of a preliminary report on the investigations; local officials contend the report was destroyed in an August 1990 fire.

Among local drug bosses rumored at the time to have ordered the slaying were Juan N. Guerra and Juan García Abrego, leaders of the so-called Gulf cartel. In January 1996, Mexican police captured García Abrego and turned him over to U.S. authorities in Texas, purportedly his place of birth. García Abrego has been accused of running a multimillion-dollar cocaine smuggling empire in the northeastern border region. He is also allegedly linked to several murders in the United States. He is being held without bail in a U.S. federal prison while he awaits trial in late 1996. Mexican authorities have not charged Guerra or García Abrego with involvement in the murders of Flores Torrijos and Moreno Figueroa.

Norma Alicia Moreno Figueroa, *El Popular*
Date of Death: July 17, 1986
Place of Death: Matamoros, Tamaulipas

M oreno Figueroa, a reporter with *El Popular* of Matamoros, Tamaulipas, was accompanying editor Ernesto Flores Torrijos when they were both killed by gunfire. Flores Torrijos is thought to have been the target of the attack.

Odilón López Urías, *Onda*
Date of Death: October 7, 1986
Place of Death: Guamuchil, Sinaloa

L ópez Urías, editor of the magazine *Onda,* was kidnapped by a group of armed men while driving with his family. His body was found on the highway outside Culiacán, Sinaloa, two days after he had been kidnapped. His magazine repeatedly had denounced local drug traffickers and related police corruption. Notorious for its large number of unsolved murders, Sinaloa has long been the homeland of Mexico's major drug trafficking rings.

1988

Manuel Burgueño Orduño, *El Sol del Pacífico*
Date of Death: January 22, 1988
Place of Death: Mazatlán, Sinaloa

B urgueño, a columnist with the daily *El Sol del Pacífico,* of Mazatlán, Sinaloa, was killed by three masked men who forced their way into his home. Burgueño frequently wrote about drugs and crime. Mazatlán, a Pacific beach resort, has also long been a center for heroin and cocaine trafficking.

Two of Burgueño's murderers, Sergio Patiño Ramírez and Antonio Cordero Lamadrid, were convicted and sentenced to 31 years and 8 months in prison. A third accused murderer, Rigoberto Rodríguez Bañuelos, was never apprehended.

Héctor Félix "El Gato" Miranda, *Zeta*
Date of Death: April 20, 1988
Place of Death: Tijuana, Baja California

Félix, a columnist and co-publisher of the muckraking weekly *Zeta* of Tijuana, Baja California, was shot to death while driving on a Tijuana highway. Felix's acerbic criticisms of powerful local politicians had made him one of the most well-known journalists in the northern border state. His avidly read columns for the Tijuana daily *ABC* a decade earlier prompted a takeover of the paper by a ruling-party-affiliated union. Félix and Jesús Blancornelas, editor of *ABC* who was fired during the takeover, co-founded the weekly *Zeta* in 1979. Some of Félix's colleagues said at the time of the murder that they suspected it had been carried out at the behest of one of Félix's frequent targets, Jorge Hank Rhon, owner of a famed Tijuana racetrack and son of a prominent Mexico City politician. Hank denied involvement.

In 1989, a former head of security at Hank's Aguacaliente racetrack, Antonio Vera Palestina, and another racetrack employee, Victoriano Medina Moreno, also a former state judicial police officer, were arrested, convicted of murder and sentenced to 27 and 25 years in prison, respectively. *Zeta* editors say Hank's involvement in the murder was never seriously investigated in deference to his political connections. Hank's father, Carlos Hank González, who became one of Mexico's wealthiest men during a long career in government, had served as both mayor of Mexico City and governor of the surrounding State of Mexico. He subsequently held several cabinet posts under Presidents Miguel de la Madrid (1982-1988) and Carlos Salinas de Gortari (1988-1994).

In July 1992, the federal government's Human Rights Commission inquired into the case. One man said to have been able to offer important testimony in the case, Emigdio Narváez, was reportedly murdered by unknown assailants shortly afterward. In 1996, CPJ, International PEN and the Inter American Press Association (IAPA) publicly backed *Zeta*'s request to the Baja California state governor that the investigation officially be reopened.

1991

Víctor Manuel Oropeza, *Diario de Juárez*, *Diario de Chihuahua*
Date of Death: July 3, 1991
Place of Death: Ciudad Juárez, Chihuahua

O ropeza, author of the daily column "My Way" for *Diario de Juárez* in Juárez, Chihuahua, was stabbed to death in his office. The assailants, however, did not touch the cash, nearly US$2000, or any other valuable items. Oropeza had written articles denouncing election fraud and the alleged murders of Indian peasants by federal drug agents. He had received death threats. The federal attorney general sent a special envoy to Chihuahua to take charge of the politically sensitive case. Rather than try to apprehend the murderers, the envoy tried to portray the victim as a homosexual and a drug dealer. Two persons who confessed to murdering Oropeza in the course of a burglary later denied the confessions and claimed they were tortured into the confessions. The attorney general for the state of Chihuahua reopened the case in July 1994, after the two suspects were freed, thanks to the efforts of the federal government's Human Rights Commission. In the summer of 1996, authorities in the state of Chihuahua said they had lost documents crucial to the case, making it impossible to continue with the investigation and identification of the authors of the crime.

1993

Roberto Mancilla Herrero, *Cuarto Poder*
Date of Death: February 2, 1993
Place of Death: Tuxtla Gutiérrez, Chiapas

M ancilla Herrero, journalist for the Chiapas newspaper *Cuarto Poder* and founding editor of *El Observador de la Frontera Sur*, was found dead in his car in Tuxtla Gutiérrez, Chiapas, shot twice in the head at close range. Local journalists believe his still-unsolved murder was linked to his investigations into possible police involvement in the murders of 11 homosexual men in Tuxtla, the Chiapas state capital. Two suspects, Esteban de Jesús Zorrilla and Vicente Espinosa Pimental, were tried and found not guilty. They declared that they had given false confessions under torture.

1995

Cuauhtémoc Ornelas Campos, *Alcance*
Missing since October 4, 1995
Place of Disappearance: Torreón, Coahuila

Ornelas Campos, editor of the monthly magazine *Alcance* in Torreón, Coahuila, disappeared after a meeting he supposedly had with Carlos López Mercado, brother of the then-mayor of Torreón. Ornelas Campos is presumed dead. The now-defunct monthly had been run by Ornelas Campos with the help of his wife and a secretary. It reprinted articles from other periodicals on drugs, official corruption and police abuses in different areas of Mexico. Although it is not known if Ornelas Campos received any threats prior to his disappearance, his media colleagues and the investigators in charge of his case believe that his disappearance is related to his journalistic work. Local journalists note that Ornelas Campos' last known appointment was with Carlos López Mercado, who had requested the appointment, reportedly to discuss *Alcance*'s allegations of municipal corruption. Police interrogated López Mercado but did not press charges. Another suspect was a federal police officer who *Alcance* had accused of involvement in drug trafficking. The police officer responded with a letter in another publication in which he accused Ornelas Campos of attempted extortion. Ornelas Campos filed a complaint with the National Human Rights Commission, which he later withdrew. After Ornelas Campos disappeared, the police officer was brought in for questioning, but no charges were filed. State investigators say that they have been unable to establish an explanation for Ornelas Campos' disappearance or identify any suspects.

Cases Under Investigation

In the following cases, CPJ has not been able to establish a clear probable link between the murder and the victim's professional work as a journalist. In each of these cases, however, friends or colleagues of the murdered journalists suspect or are firmly convinced that such a linkage exists. Difficulties in determining a probable motive or in establishing basic facts surrounding the deaths are in most cases a consequence of cursory or contradictory investigative reports by state prosecutors and local and state police.

1985

Emilio Santiago Alvarado, *Portavoz*
Date of Death: March 6, 1985
Place of Death: Tehuacán, Puebla

S antiago Alvarado, a photographer for the local weekly *Portavoz*, was shot
to death while driving in his car in Tehuacán, Puebla. Colleagues and
relatives speculated that Santiago Alvarado could have been mistaken for his
brother, the editor-in-chief of *Portavoz*, which was known for its critical
coverage of local government. Local papers reported that two suspects, whom
they identified, had been detained by police for questioning. Neither the state
prosecutor of Puebla nor the federal government's Human Rights Commission
has any information about the reported interrogation or the alleged suspects.
No charges were filed in connection with the murder.

1987

Jesús Michel Jacobo, *El Sol de Sinaloa*
Date of Death: December 16, 1987
Place of Death: Sinaloa

J acobo wrote about drug trafficking and other issues as a columnist for the
daily *El Sol de Sinaloa* and the magazine *Zeta*. He was shot to death by
unidentified gunmen while driving his car. Jacobo also was a lawyer who
reportedly defended accused drug traffickers.

1988

Ronay González Reyes, *El Mundo*
Date of Death: July 13, 1988
Place of Death: Comitán de Domínguez, Chiapas

G onzález Reyes, editor of the newspaper *El Mundo*, was shot to death in
his office in Comitán de Domínguez, state of Chiapas. Local newspapers
reported that González Reyes had received several threats prior to his
assassination. A report by Comitán's public prosecutor and the police of the
state of Chiapas asserted that the murder was provoked by a personal dispute
between two families. Some local journalists disputed the report, saying that
they suspected that González Reyes was killed because of *El Mundo*'s
reporting. No one has been arrested or charged with the killing.

Linda Bejarano, Channel 44-TV and XHGU-FM radio
Date of Death: July 23, 1988
Place of Death: Ciudad Juárez, Chihuahua

Bejarano, a broadcast reporter and commentator for XHIJ-TV (Channel 44) and XHGU-FM radio in Ciudad Juárez, Chihuahua, was shot to death at 3:00 am in a police ambush with her mother-in-law, Lucrecia Martínez, and a family friend, Carlos García. Her husband, Manuel Gómez Martínez, a journalist who also worked for the same television and radio stations, was the only survivor of the fusillade. The victims were sitting in their parked car when a group of 15 plainclothes federal judicial police agents opened fire from two nearby police vans. Gómez and others reported that they tried to drive away but were pursued, still under fire from the police. The car stalled after gunshots killed García, the driver, and perforated the gas tank. Gómez says he was spared assassination for still-uncertain reasons while his wife and mother-in-law were killed at point-blank range.

Police later claimed that they mistook Bejarano's car for one with a similar description owned by reputed drug traffickers that they had been pursuing. Gómez disputes this mistaken-identity defense and speculates that they were attacked deliberately because they were reporters known to have information on federal police collusion with drug trafficking in the border city. Neither Bejarano nor Gómez had done such broadcast reporting, however. Felipe García Martínez, Raúl Salinas García, Joaquín García Méndez, Santos Robles Peña, Roberto Gómez Silguero and Noé Librado Zavala were each found guilty of the murders and were sentenced to between 25 and 27 years in prison. After filing appeals, all obtained lesser sentences and were released from prison in 1995.

1990

Alfredo Córdova Solórzano, *Unomásdos*
Date of Death: June 9, 1990
Place of Death: Tapachula, Chiapas

Córdova Solórzano, editor-in-chief of the daily *Unomásdos* and a correspondent for the Mexico City daily *Excélsior* and the Tuxtla Gutiérrez daily *La República* in Chiapas, died on June 9, three days after he was shot by unidentified gunmen in his home in the city of Tapachula. Colleagues in the Chiapas southern border town said they suspected that his death was related to his newspaper's coverage of drug trafficking. There have been no prosecutions connected with the case.

1992

Ignacio Mendoza Castillo, *La Voz del Caribe*
Date of Death: November 13, 1992
Place of Death: Mexico City, Mexico

M endoza Castillo, editor and publisher of the magazine *La Voz del Caribe*, from the state of Quintana Roo, was shot to death in Mexico City. Two days before, he had staged a protest demonstration outside the annual "National Press Day" luncheon, which featured a speech by President Salinas de Gortari, to complain of harassment and intimidation by local authorities in his home state. A suspect was apprehended and confessed to the crime, claiming that he killed Mendoza Castillo because of a financial dispute unrelated to the journalist's work. The accused gunman later recanted, saying his testimony had been extracted under police torture. An Inter American Press Association delegation led by Monterrey publisher Alejandro Junco traveled to Quintana Roo to investigate the case but was unable to corroborate Mendoza Castillo's original accusations or to link his death to his journalism activities.

1993

Jessica Elizalde de León, *El Fronterizo*
Date of Death: March 15, 1993
Place of Death: Ciudad Juárez, Chihuahua

E lizalde de León, a journalist for the local dailies *El Fronterizo* and *El Tiempo*, Radio Centro and 106 FM radio station, was shot twice in the face and killed at her home in Ciudad Juárez, Chihuahua. The crime does not appear to have been related to journalism. Sources say de León had been an undercover informant for U.S. and Mexican police agencies investigating Elías Ramírez, a drug trafficker and former commander of the judicial state police of Chihuahua.

Araceli Caballero, *El Día*
Date of Death: June 6, 1993
Place of Death: Ecatepec, Mexico State

Caballero, a correspondent for the Mexico City daily *El Día*, was found dead in her car with a bullet in her head in the town of Ecatepec in the state of Mexico. Caballero reportedly had received threats from local officials after publishing a series of articles on alleged fraud in municipal land sales. Ricardo Palomino Huerta, a suspected thief, was charged with the crime. Police said the motive for the murder was robbery.

1994

Jorge Martín Dorantes, *El Crucero de la Ciudad*
Date of Death: June 6, 1994
Place of Death: Cuernavaca, Morelos

Unknown assailants shot and killed Dorantes, editor and founder of the weekly *El Crucero de la Ciudad*, published in Cuernavaca, Morelos. He was a known critic of local government officials, although some colleagues said the paper existed largely to collect money from the state by selling ads and being subsidized. On May 24, 1995, an acquaintance of Dorantes, Arthur Paul Ruggeberg Barber, was charged with the murder. An arrest warrant was issued, but Ruggeberg Barber reportedly had fled. A report by the state prosecutor alleged that Dorantes had had an affair with Ruggeberg's wife. Colleagues blamed the police for neglecting leads that they said could produce a link between Dorantes' professional work and the crime. Dorantes was the first of three journalists murdered in Morelos in a six-week period.

Enrique Peralta Torres, *La Unión*
Date of Death: July 6, 1994
Place of Death: Jojutlá, Morelos

Peralta Torres was the second journalist from the Morelos region to be killed within a month. He had worked for the Morelos newspaper *La Unión* until March when he was asked to resign due to a rising conflict of interests over his acceptance of a government position. He died from multiple gunshot wounds but was reportedly able to identify his assassin as Fidencio Muñoz Malpica, a business associate who has since fled the country. No one has been arrested or charged in the murder.

José Luis Rojas, *La Unión*
Date of Death: July 11, 1994
Place of Death: Chamilpa City, Morelos

Rojas, a reporter for the Morelos newspaper *La Unión*, was found strangled to death on July 13. He was the second journalist from the newspaper killed in less than a week and the third journalist murdered in the state in a two-month period. Although not known for critical or controversial writing, he was one of the best-known journalists in Morelos. In late July, police issued an arrest warrant for Israel Ríos Lavín, a suspect, and in August, they arrested Emi Carlos Ayala, Lavín's alleged accomplice, and accused him of disposing of the victim's body. Ayala claimed that the death was an accident. Lavín has not been apprehended. According to the government's Human Rights Commission, local official investigators termed the killing a "homosexual crime of passion." (Though the facts in this case remain unclear, it should be noted that this is a common allegation in Mexican police investigations of the deaths of journalists and political activists. Critics say its intended effect is to discourage relatives and colleagues from publicly demanding further investigations.)

1995

Ruperto Armenta Gerardo, *El Regional*
Date of Death: February 5, 1995
Place of Death: Guasave, Sinaloa

A rmenta, editor of the Guasave-based weekly *El Regional* in the state of Sinaloa, was beaten to death by the lawyer Felipe de Jesús Lizárraga and his body dumped in a canal near Guasave. Lizárraga, who was an acquaintance of Armenta and was driving with him in the car found at the scene, claimed that they had been attacked by police agents. Because of contradictions in his statement and other evidence, Lizárraga was charged with the murder and detained, but the then-president of the Lawyers' Guild of Sinaloa was freed, setting off demonstrations by journalists who believed he had killed Armenta after a fight over articles the journalist had written about him. As a result of the demonstrations, Lizárraga was arrested again and tried. On November 18, he was convicted and sentenced to 13 years and three months in prison and fined 11,000 nuevos pesos. Lizárraga has appealed the sentence.

Index

Production Notes

This book was printed on 60 lb. Glatfelter Natural text with a 10 point CIS cover stock.

The text and index of this volume, designed by Susan Kay Holler, were set in Garamond at the North-South Center Press, using Aldus PageMaker 4.2, on a Power Macintosh 8500/120 computer.

The cover was created by Mary M. Mapes using QuarkXpress 3.32.

Jayne M. Weisblatt, senior editor, and Kathleen A. Hamman, editorial director, copy edited the book. Mary D'León, editorial research coordinator, proofread the book and ensured accurate spelling of Spanish-language terms.

This publication was printed by Edwards Brothers, Inc. of Lillington, North Carolina, USA.